1st Workshop on Creative-text Translation and Technology (CTT 2024)

Sheffield, United Kingdom
27 June 2024

ISBN: 979-8-3313-0478-2

Printed from e-media with permission by:

Curran Associates, Inc.
57 Morehouse Lane
Red Hook, NY 12571

Association for Computational Linguistics
209 N. Eighth Street
Stroudsburg, Pennsylvania 18360

Phone: 1-570-476-8006
Fax: 1-570-476-0860

acl@aclweb.org

Additional copies of this publication are available from:

Curran Associates, Inc.
57 Morehouse Lane
Red Hook, NY 12571 USA
Phone: 845-758-0400
Fax: 845-758-2633
Email: curran@proceedings.com
Web: www.proceedings.com

CTT 2024

The 1st Workshop on Creative-text Translation and Technology

Proceedings

June 27, 2024

The CTT organizers gratefully acknowledge the support from the following sponsors.

With the support of

Preface by the Workshop Organizers

This volume contains the contributions to the first workshop on Creative-text Translation and Technology (CTT).[1] CTT is co-located with the 25th Annual Conference of the European Association for Machine Translation (EAMT 2024)[2], held on 27 June 2024 in Sheffield, UK.

Scope. In an era where technological advances continuously reshape the potential of language tools, the call for papers asked for novel work that discusses the creative aspects of language technology. Our scope was therefore deliberately broad, envisioning work on the use of language technology for the translation of texts in creative domains, such as marketing, literature and poetry, audiovisual translation, and multilingual content creation. Tools could include large language models (LLMs), computer-aided translation (CAT) tools, machine translation (MT) systems, post-editing environments, and so on. Furthermore, we aimed to attract submissions from a diverse range of profiles: researchers, educators, translators and industry stakeholders were all encouraged to submit their work to ensure a broad platform for discussion focused on the suitability of current language technology for different creative translation processes.

Submissions. We received 9 submissions in total. After a double-blind peer-review process, two papers were rejected because their focus on language technology was too limited in scope. We encouraged those authors to submit their work to more topical venues. With 7 out of 9 papers ultimately accepted, we have an acceptance rate of 78%, with an average reviewer score of 16/20. All papers are between 5 and 9 pages long and accepted for oral presentation.
Given the current technological landscape, it does not come as a surprise that LLMs emerged as a topic of significant interest. Van Egdom, Declercq, & Kosters investigate how post-editing through prompting can improve the quality of machine-translated literary work. Macken presents a study that compares the quality of professional (human) post-editing and post-editing with ChatGPT in a selection of short stories. And Castaldo & Monti focus on a specific type of creative language translation, namely idioms, and analyse the quality of LLMs when translating these expressions.
With regards to workflows, Daems, Ruffo, & Macken compare the effect of using different types of translation workspaces (Word, Trados, and a literary post-editing platform) on translation text features, such as sentence length and style, in the context of short story translation. Oliver & Alvarez-Vidal report on the LitPC toolkit, a set of tools that can aid in building parallel corpora from literary works, which in turn can be used to train machine translation systems. Mikelenić & Oliver introduce neural MT systems tailored to literature in Spanish, French, Italian, Portuguese and Romanian, leveraging both multilingual literary corpora and web-crawled datasets. And Jon & Bojar investigate surprisal distributions in the source text on the one hand and MT and human translation on the other, hypothesising that MT models enforce a uniform surprisal distribution.

Keynotes. We have the pleasure to host two keynote speakers at CTT.[3] Ana Guerberof Arenas will present the work done on creativity in machine translation and beyond in her past project CREAMT and her newly-acquired ERC project INCREC. Andrew Rothwell will discuss how literary translators can "augment" their creativity in this fast-changing technological landscape while providing an overview of the various technological tools that are available.

Sponsors. CTT is grateful to be sponsored by INTERACT: Interdisciplinary research network on language contact research[4], funded by the Research Foundation Flanders with grant number W002220N.

[1] https://ctt2024.ccl.kuleuven.be/
[2] https://eamt2024.sheffield.ac.uk/
[3] https://ctt2024.ccl.kuleuven.be/keynotes
[4] https://interact.ugent.be/

CTT is also sponsored by the research group on Computational and Formal Linguistics (ComForT)[5] at KU Leuven.

With this first workshop on Creative-text Translation and Technology, we aim to bring together a diverse audience to talk about the applicability of language technology to creative-text translation. We are looking forward to the fruitful discussions and insights.

June 2024,
Bram Vanroy, Marie-Aude Lefer, Lieve Macken, Paola Ruffo

[5] https://www.arts.kuleuven.be/ling/comfort-english/

Organizing Committee

Program Chairs

Bram Vanroy, Instituut voor de Nederlandse Taal and KU Leuven
Marie-Aude Lefer, UCLouvain
Lieve Macken, Universiteit Gent
Paola Ruffo, Universiteit Gent

Program Committee

Reviewers

Lynne Bowker, University of Ottawa
Joke Daems, Universiteit Gent
Ana Guerberof-Arenas, University of Groningen
James Luke Hadley, University of Dublin, Trinity College
Damien Hansen, University of Liège
Alina Karakanta, Leiden University
Dorothy Kenny, Dublin City University
Waltraud Kolb, University of Vienna
Maarit Koponen, University of Eastern Finland
Antoni Oliver, Universitat Oberta de Catalunya
Paola Ruffo, Universiteit Gent
Minna Ruokonen, University of Eastern Finland
Kristiina Taivalkoski-Shilov, University of Turku
Arda Tezcan, Universiteit Gent
Antonio Toral, University of Groningen
Susana Valdez, Universiteit Leiden
Chantal Wright, ZHAW - Zürcher Hochschule für Angewandte Wissenschaften
Mehmet Şahin, Boğaziçi University

Keynote Talk
The INCREC project: creativity and technology in translation

Ana Guerberof Arenas
University of Groningen, The Netherlands

Thu, June 27, 2024 – Time: **09:00 – 10:00** –

Abstract: In this talk, I will give an overview of how creativity is conceptualised in the social sciences, mainly psychology and sociology, including different frameworks that facilitate analysing creativity. I will also touch upon how the technological field has presented and has studied creativity, and how translation in combination with technology can be explored.
With this aim in mind, I will also present results from the CREAMT project (2020-2022) that explored creativity in literary texts in different translation modalities: translation by professional literary translators, machine translation using a customized neural engine, and post-edition. Further it looked at the impact on readers by looking at narrative engagement, enjoyment and translation reception.
Finally, I will describe the new ERC CoG INCREC research project (2023-2028) that looks to uncover the creative process in professional literary and audiovisual translators in order to create specific frameworks, and how and when technology, e.g. machine translation, can be used to enhance rather than constrain creativity. But also if the intended audiences, readers and viewers, appreciate, not only cognitively but also emotionally, creative shifts in translated content and why this might be.

Bio: Ana Guerberof Arenas is an associate professor in Translation Studies at University of Groningen. From 2020-22, she was a Marie Skłodowska Curie Research Fellow working on the CREAMT project that looked at the impact of MT on translation creativity and the reader's experience in the context of literary texts. More recently she has been awarded a ERC Consolidator grant by the European Research Council to work on the five-year project INCREC (2023-2028) that explores the translation creative process in its intersect with technology in literary and AVT translation. She has authored refereed articles and book chapters on MT post-editing; reading comprehension of MT output; translator training, ethical considerations in MT, AI and the industry, creativity and reception studies. She has more than 23 years' experience in the translation industry.

Keynote Talk
CAT, TM, NMT, and AI: A Literary Translator's Dream Team?

Andrew Rothwell
Swansea University, United Kingdom

Thu, June 27, 2024 – Time: **13:30 – 14:30** –

Abstract: Since the public release of ChatGPT in November 2022, there has been an explosion of interest in the remarkable text-production capabilities (including paraphrasing, summarizing and translation) of such generative AI tools. Whether they can be of assistance to the literary translator, and if so, how they can best be made to interoperate with existing CAT and MT environments, remains, however, a largely moot question.
This paper will describe my developing use of different technologies, over almost a decade, to produce English translations of classic novels in French by Emile Zola and Marcel Proust. Acknowledging the documented reticence of literary translators to adopt computerised tools, I will nevertheless argue for the practical benefits of using: –

- an electronic ST
- aligned bilingual editor (aka CAT tool)
- translation memory
- termbase
- online dictionaries and thesauri
- NMT (free-standing and CAT-integrated)
- generative AI.

The core of the paper will be a presentation of how these technologies are now being combined in a single interface, taking as an example the recently AI-enhanced CAT tool Wordscope. Wordscope offers an integration of translation memory, machine translation from several providers, and ChatGPT as a research and paraphrasing tool, in a de-cluttered online environment.
The paper will describe different options for using the tool for literary translation, and discuss some theoretical implications of doing so in a Cognitive Translation Studies framework. In conclusion, I will argue

that Lommel's (2018) notion that the translator's creative capacity is 'augmented' rather than inhibited by computer technologies applies no less to literary than to 'commercial' translation, albeit in significantly different ways.

Bio: Andrew Rothwell is Emeritus Professor of French and Translation Studies at Swansea University. He has research interests in contemporary French literature, especially the poet and art writer Bernard Noël, translation technologies, and translation theory. He has published numerous literary translations into English, including of poetry by Noël and two novels by Emile Zola (for Oxford World's Classics), and is currently working on a new translation of Marcel Proust's *La Prisonnière* for the same publisher. Recent books include *Translation Tools and Technologies* (with Joss Moorkens, María Fernández Parra, Joanna Drugan and Frank Austermuehl) and *Computer-Assisted Literary Translation* (co-edited with Andy Way and Roy Youdale), both published in 2023 by Routledge.

Table of Contents

Using a multilingual literary parallel corpus to train NMT systems

Bojana Mikelenić
University of Zagreb
bmikelen@ffzg.unizg.hr

Antoni Oliver
Universitat Oberta de Catalunya
aoliverg@uoc.edu

Abstract

This article presents an application of a multilingual and multidirectional parallel corpus composed of literary texts in five Romance languages (Spanish, French, Italian, Portuguese, Romanian) and a Slavic language (Croatian), with a total of 142,000 segments and 15.7 million words. After combining it with very large freely available parallel corpora, this resource is used to train NMT systems tailored to literature. A total of five NMT systems have been trained: Spanish-French, Spanish-Italian, Spanish-Portuguese, Spanish-Romanian and Spanish-Croatian. The trained systems were evaluated using automatic metrics (BLEU, chrF2 and TER) and a comparison with a rule-based MT system (Apertium) and a neural system (Google Translate) is presented. As a main conclusion, we can highlight that the use of this literary corpus has been very productive, as the majority of the trained systems achieve comparable, and in some cases even better, values of the automatic quality metrics than a widely used commercial NMT system.

1 Introduction

Parallel multilingual corpora have a wide use and are known for their application in different kinds of linguistic research (contrastive linguistics, translation studies, phraseology, lexicography, etc.) (Lefer, 2021), translation training (López Rodríguez, 2016) and training of machine translation systems (Koehn et al., 2007; Koehn, 2020), as well as terminology extraction (Lefever et al., 2009).

The parallel corpus RomCro (Bikić-Carić et al., 2023) was created taking into account all these possible applications. This project started in autumn 2019 and it is financed by the Faculty of Humanities and Social Sciences of the University of Zagreb. RomCro is a multilingual and multidirectional parallel corpus, which is aligned and annotated with MSD (Morpho-Syntactic Description) tags. It is composed of original literary texts written in five Romance languages (Spanish, French, Italian, Portuguese, Romanian) as well as Croatian, and their respective published translations into the other five languages. Even though lemmatization and annotation are not relevant for the task at hand, they were completed in order to allow for different uses of the corpus, such as extracting desired structures and their translations for contrastive analysis or translator training.

Most previous studies about machine translation (MT) of literary texts are quite recent (from 2012 onwards). According to Toral and Way (2015), a key challenge in literary translation is preserving not only the meaning, but also the reading experience. This is a key difference to other domains, for example, technical or legal texts. Hansen and Esperanza-Rodier (2022) evaluate a customized MT system tailored for a literary translator specializing in fiction. The study demonstrates that fine-tuning a base model with a smaller subset of custom training data can yield translations closer to human references, despite the raw output still falling short of human quality. Other studies (Oliver, 2023) also suggest the idea of training author-tailored NMT systems for literary texts.

Proceedings of the 1st Workshop on Creative-text Translation and Technology, pages 1–9
June 27, 2024 ©2024 European Association for Machine Translation

Most of the studies remark the idea that translation technologies are still not mature enough for translation of literary works ready to be published and that human translators are needed for this task. Bur NMT systems for literary works can still have several interesting uses, as for example (1) produce draft translation for editorial teams to decide whether to publish a translation of a novel in a given market, promoting the cultural interchange and the visibility of authors writing in smaller languages; (2) produce bilingual electronic books where users can access the translation of difficult sentences or paragraphs, promoting reading in the original language, among others.

We will dedicate the first part of this paper to describe the corpus RomCro, in order to understand its characteristics as well as the process of its creation, and then proceed to explore its application in Neural Machine Translation (NMT).

2 Building RomCro

The corpus contains 27 original titles: seven in Spanish, six in French, four in Italian, four in Romanian, three in Portuguese and three in Croatian, as it is shown in Table 1 (including the author and the year of publication). Adding the translation to all the other languages, that makes 162 texts in total. However, there are three translated texts that are not yet available[1] and two that were acquired and added recently[2] only to the version of the corpus available through Sketch Engine (Kilgarriff et al., 2008). The version of the corpus used in this experiment does not include these five texts, so it contains 157 texts, counting the originals and their translations. The total number of translation units is 142,470, and the total number of words is 15.7 million. The distribution by language in millions of words is as follows: French 2.8, Spanish 2.7, Romanian 2.6, Italian 2.6, Portuguese 2.6, and Croatian 2.4.

There were six stages in building the corpus: 1) Selection and collection of texts, 2) Digitization of texts, 3) Preparation for segmentation and sentence alignment, 4) Segmentation, alignment and manual correction, 5) Lemmatization and morphosyntactic annotation (with MSD tags), and 6) Access to the corpus.

One of the main challenges was to find high quality material translated from the original language into the rest of the languages, which is why literary texts were chosen. The uneven divide between the number of originals in each language (Table 1) is due to a higher availability of titles translated from some languages (e.g., Spanish) then other, smaller ones (e.g., Croatian). In order to keep the corpus as synchronic as possible, the texts should have been published relatively recently. This was more difficult for some languages, namely Romanian, where two titles from the first half of the 20th century had to be selected. To maintain homogeneity in the corpus, the inclusion of exclusively European varieties of Spanish, French and Portuguese was preferred. However, since four titles were translated only into Brazilian Portuguese,[3] they were added to the corpus with a possibility of excluding them when consulting it, filtering by notes provided in each segment.

Once the selection of texts was completed, digitization of those not available in digital format was initiated. They were scanned and then an Optical Character Recognition using Abbyy FineReader was performed.

In the next stage, the material was prepared for segmentation and alignment by manually correcting texts in MS Word. Several undergraduate and master level students collaborated on the project, reviewing and correcting the results of this digitization, that is, preparing the texts for automatic alignment.

The segmentation and alignment was performed using LF Aligner,[4] a freely available tool based on Hunalign (Varga et al., 2005). The results were again revised and corrected manually.

The lemmatization and morphosyntactic annotation was done using the annotators available via Sketch Engine, which were FreeLing (Padró, 2011) for Spanish, French, Italian and Portuguese, and MULTEXT-East (Erjavec et al., 2003; Erjavec, 2017) for Romanian and Croatian.

A lemmatized and POS tagged version of the corpus containing 159 texts is available on Sketch Engine. For direct access to the untagged TMX and TSV versions used in this experiment (com-

[1]The book *El asombroso viaje de Pomponio Flato* is not available in Romanian, while *Dora i Minotaur: Moj život s Picassom* is still not translated to Spanish and Portuguese.

[2]These are the Portuguese translation of *Maitreyi* and the Italian translation of *Muzej bezuvjetne predaje*.

[3]The texts are as follows: *A fada carabina* by Daniel Pennac, *A forma da água* by Andrea Camilleri, *Acontecimentos na Irrealidade Imediata* by Max Blecher and *Nostalgia* by Mircea Cărtărescu.

[4]`https://sourceforge.net/projects/aligner/`

n.	Lang.	Titles:
1	ES	La sombra del viento (C.R. Zafón, 2001)
2		La catedral del mar (I. Falcones, 2006)
3		El juego del ángel (C.R. Zafón, 2008)
4		El asombroso viaje de Pomponio Flato (E. Mendoza, 2008)
5		Soldados de Salamina (J. Cercas, 2001)
6		El mapa del tiempo (F. J. Palma, 2008)
7		El tiempo entre costuras (M. Dueñas, 2009)
8	FR	Seras-tu là ? (G. Musso, 2006)
9		HHhH (L. Binet, 2010)
10		Un barrage contre le Pacifique (M. Duras, 1950)
11		La Fée Carabine (D. Pennac, 1987)
12		L'amant (M. Duras, 1984)
13		A l'ombre des jeunes filles en fleur (M. Proust, 1919)
14	IT	Imprimatur (Monaldi & Sorti, 2002)
15		Le otto montagne (P. Cognetti, 2017)
16		La forma dell'acqua (A. Camilleri, 1994)
17		L'amica geniale (E. Ferrante, 2011)
18	RO	Maitreyi (M. Eliade, 1933)
19		Întâmplări în irealitatea imediată (M. Blecher, 1936)
20		Nostalgia (M. Cărtărescu, 1993)
21		Cartea şoaptelor (V. Vosganian, 2009)
22	PT	A viagem do elefante (J. Saramago, 2008)
23		Nenhum olhar (J. L. Peixoto, 2000)
24		As intermitências da morte (J. Saramago, 2005)
25	HR	Muzej bezuvjetne predaje (D. Ugrešić, 1998)
26		Mediteranski brevijar (P. Matvejević, 1987)
27		Dora i Minotaur: Moj život s Picassom (S. Drakulić, 2015)

Table 1: A list of the original titles in the corpus

prising 157 texts) under the CC-BY-NC-4.0 license, please refer to the ELRC (European Language Resource Coordination) platform.[5] In both formats, the order of languages is Spanish (es), French (fr), Italian (it), Portuguese (pt), Romanian (ro), Croatian (hr). All the versions of the corpus contain notes about the original language, writer, and the original title of the text the segment is from. Additionally, segment order was scrambled to protect copyright.

3 Comparison to similar corpora

Many parallel corpora are freely available on the Internet. The main collection can be found in Opus Corpora (Tiedemann, 2012). However, only a minority of these parallel corpora are created from literary texts, and when available, they do not contain many parallel segments (for example Books[6]), or are created from individual or a small number of works (as Salome[7]).

To the best of our knowledge, this is the first multilingual and almost completely multidirectional parallel corpus that aligns literary texts in several Romance languages and one Slavic. In other similar corpora, the Slavic language was the pivot language (Terzić et al., 2020; Grabar et al., 2018; Akimova et al., 2020), which means that all texts were translated from or to the Slavic language, but not necessarily between each other.

Croatian is present in some multilingual literary corpora, such as TransLiTex (Fraisse et al., 2018) or InterCorp (Čermák, 2019), which also includes literary texts. However, TransLiTex contains translations of a single book into 23 languages and InterCorp is made up of 40 languages, including all

[5] `https://elrc-share.eu/repository/search/?q=romcro`

[6] `https://opus.nlpl.eu/Books.php`

[7] `https://opus.nlpl.eu/Salome-v1.php`

those that form part of RomCro, but has Czech as the pivot language.

4 Using RomCro to train NMT systems tailored to literary texts

As an example of use of RomCro, we explore the training of Neural Machine Translation systems tailored to literature. A total of five NMT systems have been trained, combining the Spanish subcorpus (original and translated material) with subcorpora in the other five languages. In other words, the trained NMT systems were Spanish to French, Italian, Portuguese, Romanian and Croatian. In this section all the processes performed to train and evaluate these systems are described.

4.1 Extending the corpus

First of all, the size of RomCro is insufficient for training these NMT systems. We have about 150,000 segments when we would require several million. To obtain the needed segments, we have combined RomCro with a very large parallel corpus, such as CCMatrix[8] (Schwenk et al., 2021) and MultiCCAligned[9] (El-Kishky et al., 2020). Unfortunately, such very large parallel corpora contain errors, as some segments are not in the correct language and some segment pairs are not translation equivalents. To solve this problem, we have rescored the parallel corpora using the MTUOC-PCorpus-rescorer[10] (Oliver and Álvarez, 2023). This tool automatically detects the language of each segment and checks if each segment pair is really a translation equivalent using SBERT[11] (Reimers and Gurevych, 2019), providing a confidence score. We have used a threshold of 0.75 for each check. In Table 2, the size in segments for the raw and rescored versions can be observed. As we can see, for all language pairs except Spanish-Croatian, we have enough segments in the rescored version.

For Spanish-Croatian we have concatenated several parallel corpora,[12] and eliminated repeated parallel segments, obtaining a corpus with 29 million parallel segments, resulting in 12.4 million after rescoring. This is the corpus that we have used combined with RomCro.

Corpus	Type	Segments	Rescored
spa-fra	CCMatrix	266.5 M	159.7 M
spa-ita	CCMatrix	142.1 M	80.9 M
spa-por	CCMatrix	198.5 M	114.4 M
spa-rom	CCMatrix	53.7 M	25.9 M
spa-cro	MultiCC Al.	2.9 M	88.5 K

Table 2: Size of the corpora before and after rescoring (in millions of segments)

Once we have obtained a curated version of the very large parallel corpora for the different language pairs, or General corpora, we needed to combine them with RomCro, that is, select a subset of the large parallel corpora containing the most similar segment pairs to the segment pairs in RomCro. To combine the corpus, we have used the MTUOC corpus combination algorithm,[13] for all language pairs except Spanish-Romanian and Spanish-Croatian. This program calculates a language model from the Spanish part of the RomCro corpus, and then, for all the segment pairs in the General corpus it calculates the perplexity of the Spanish part using the calculated language model. Then we can select a given number, 20 million in our experiments, of segments with the lowest perplexity. These segments are in a certain way the most similar to those in the RomCro corpus. For Spanish-Romanian and Spanish-Croatian all the available parallel segments after rescoring have been used, so this step was omitted. The training corpus contains some segments from RomCro and some from the General corpus. We assigned a weight of 1 to the segments coming from RomCro and a weight of 0.5 to those coming from the General corpus. These weights were used in the training process, giving greater importance to segments from the literary data. Please note that all the segments for the validation and evaluation corpus come from the RomCro corpus.

4.2 Training NMT systems

We have used Marian[14] (Junczys-Dowmunt et al., 2018) to train general and tailored to literature systems from Spanish to French, Italian, Portuguese, Romanian and Croatian. For the general sys-

[8] `https://github.com/facebookresearch/LASER/tree/main/tasks/CCMatrix`

[9] `https://www.statmt.org/cc-aligned/`

[10] `https://github.com/mtuoc/MTUOC-PCorpus-rescorer`

[11] `https://www.sbert.net/`

[12] MultiCCAligned, MultiParaCrawl, OpenSubtitles and ELRC-4236.

[13] `https://github.com/mtuoc/MTUOC-corpus-combination`

[14] `https://marian-nmt.github.io/`

tem we have used 20 million segments from the rescored corpus, except for Spanish-Romanian, where the whole 25.9M segments after rescoring have been used; and Spanish-Croatian, where we have used the whole concatenated corpus after rescoring consisting of 12.4M segments. The systems tailored to literature have been trained with the corpora described in the section 4.1. These systems were compared with Apertium[15] (Forcada et al., 2011), when available, and Google Translate,[16] as described below.

The training has been performed using mariannmt with a transformer configuration, using SentencePiece[17] (Kudo and Richardson, 2018) as a subword tokenizer. The weights from the combination step have been used for training.

4.3 Evaluation of the trained NMT systems

In tables 3 to 7 we present the evaluation figures for all the MT systems under study for the language pairs from Spanish to the rest of the currently available languages in RomCro. The evaluation has been performed using Sacrebleu[18] (Post, 2018): BLEU (Papineni et al., 2002), chrF2 (Popović, 2015) and TER (Snover et al., 2006). The Appendix A shows the signatures of the three metrics stating the exact configuration parameters as reported by Sacrebleu. We did not use neural evaluation metrics as COMET (Rei et al., 2020) or BLEURT (Sellam et al., 2020), as these metrics are very dependent of the used model and can give different results for different language pairs, making the results difficult to compare between the studied language pairs. For all language pairs, an evaluation set has been extracted from the RomCro corpus. The segments used in these evaluation sets have been randomly selected and they are not present in the training set nor in the validation set. We have translated these evaluation sets with all the MT systems under study, namely:

- Apertium for those language pairs with an available Apertium system: Spanish-French, Spanish-Italian and Spanish-Portuguese.
- Marian Generic: trained with 20 million segments from the General corpus (except for Spanish-Romanian and Spanish-Croatian, as explained in subsection 4.2).
- Marian RomCro: trained with RomCro and the 20 million segments most similar to RomCro selected from the General corpus (except for Spanish-Romanian and Spanish-Croatian, as explained in subsection 4.2).
- Google Translate through its Python API (Translations with Google Translate were performed between July 21-25, 2023).

For each language pair the values of BLEU, chrF2 and TER for all the evaluated systems are presented. Best values for each metric and language pair are marked in bold in the tables. In the same table, significance figures for the comparison of the Marian Generic and Marian RomCro, on one hand, and for Marian RomCro and Google Translate, on the other hand, are presented. These figures have been calculated with paired bootstrap resampling test with 1,000 resampling trials, using the -paired-bs option in Sacrebleu. In this way, one of the systems is pairwise compared to the system considered as the baseline (indicated with a B in the tables). Assuming a significance threshold of 0.05, the null hypothesis can be rejected for p-values < 0.05 (marked with "*" in the tables), indicating that the differences are significant and are not produced by chance.

In Table 3 the evaluation figures for the Spanish-French language pair can be observed. First of all and for all language pairs having Apertium, any neural system achieves better results than this transfer system. For Spanish-French the Marian RomCro achieves slightly better, but statistically significant results for BLEU (an increase of 1.3 points) and TER (a decrease of 1.8 poins) than the Marian Generic. Comparing Marian RomCro and Google Translate, the latter achieves better results in all metrics, but this difference is only significant for chrF2 (with an increase of 1.1 points).

In Table 4 the evaluation figures for Spanish-Italian are shown. For this language pair, training with RomCro is very productive, as this system achieves significantly better results than Marian Generic and Google Translate. For BLEU we get an improvement of 7.5 points with respect to Marian Generic and 1.4 with respect to Google Translate.

In Table 5 the evaluation results for the Spanish-Portuguese language pair are presented. This language pair presents a similar behaviour to Spanish-Italian, with the Marian RomCro system getting

[15]https://www.apertium.org/
[16]https://translate.google.com/
[17]https://github.com/google/sentencepiece
[18]https://github.com/mjpost/sacrebleu

System	BLEU	chrF2	TER
Apertium es-fr	19.4	49.5	72.3
Marian Generic es-fr	31.9	57.2	58.9
Marian RomCro es-fr	33.2	56.9	**57.1**
GoogleT es-fr	**33.5**	**58.0**	57.4

System	BLEU (μ ± 95% CI)	chrF2 (μ ± 95% CI)	TER (μ ± 95% CI)
B: Marian Generic es-fr	31.9 (31.9 ± 1.3)	57.2 (57.2 ± 1.0)	58.9 (58.9 ± 1.5)
Marian RomCro es-fr	**33.2 (33.2 ± 1.4) (p = 0.0020)***	56.9 (56.9 ± 1.0) (p = 0.1179)	**57.1 (57.0 ± 1.4) (p = 0.0010)***
B: Marian RomCro es-fr	33.2 (33.2 ± 1.4)	56.9 (56.9 ± 1.0)	57.1 (57.0 ± 1.4)
GoogleT es-fr	33.5 (33.4 ± 1.4) (p = 0.2118)	**58.0 (58.0 ± 0.9) (p = 0.0030)***	57.4 (57.4 ± 1.5) (p = 0.1918)

Table 3: Evaluation results for Spanish-French

System	BLEU	chrF2	TER
Apertium es-it	20.3	50.6	68.3
Marian Generic es-it	25.5	56.3	67.1
Marian RomCro es-t	**33.0**	**58.7**	**56.3**
GoogleT es-it	31.6	57.6	57.4

System	BLEU (μ ± 95% CI)	chrF2 (μ ± 95% CI)	TER (μ ± 95% CI)
B: Marian Generic es-it	25.5 (25.5 ± 1.4)	56.3 (56.3 ± 1.1)	67.1 (67.1 ± 3.0)
Marian RomCro es-it	**33.0 (32.9 ± 1.4) (p = 0.0010)***	**58.7 (58.6 ± 1.0) (p = 0.0010)***	**56.3 (56.3 ± 1.5) (p = 0.0010)***
B: Marian RomCro es-it	**33.0 (32.9 ± 1.4)**	**58.7 (58.6 ± 1.0)**	**56.3 (56.3 ± 1.5)**
GoogleT es-it	31.6 (31.6 ± 1.3) (p = 0.0030)*	57.6 (57.6 ± 1.0) (p = 0.0010)*	57.4 (57.4 ± 1.5) (p = 0.0170)*

Table 4: Evaluation results for Spanish-Italian

even better results and outperforming the Marian Generic and Google Translate. For this language pair Google Translate is getting worse results than the Marian Generic (with 5.5 less BLEU points) and Marian RomCro (with 7.1 less BLEU points).

For the Spanish-Romanian language pair (see Table 6), the Marian RomCro again outperforms the Marian Generic systems, and achieves very similar scores to Google Translate. In fact, Google Translate only gets significantly better results for the chrF2 measure (an increment of 0.7 points). For this language pair, all the parallel segments available after rescoring have been used, meaning no corpus combination was performed. This suggests that the results could potentially improve if segments more similar to RomCro could have been selected.

For the Spanish-Croatian language pair (Table 7) our training systems are getting bad results for all the metrics, very far from the values obtained for Google Translate (a decrement of 8.2 BLEU points). This should be due to the small size of the training parallel corpus and the missing corpus combination step. Even so, the use of RomCro improves significantly the results of the Generic MT engine (with an increment of 2 BLEU points).

As a general conclusion from the evaluation, we can confirm that the use of RomCro to create neural machine translation tailored to literature is promising. But there is still a lot of work to be done. Further training experiments should be performed, using some known techniques to further

System	BLEU	chrF2	TER
Apertium es-pt	31.7	58.9	53.9
Marian Generic es-pt	36.4	61.1	51.4
Marian RomCro es-pt	**38.0**	**61.9**	**49.2**
GoogleT es-pt	30.9	57.4	55.8

System	BLEU (μ ± 95% CI)	chrF2 (μ ± 95% CI)	TER (μ ± 95% CI)
B: Marian Generic es-pt	36.4 (36.3 ± 1.5)	61.1 (61.1 ± 1.0)	51.4 (51.4 ± 1.6)
Marian RomCro es-pt	**38.0 (38.0 ± 1.5) (p = 0.0010)***	**61.9 (61.9 ± 1.1) (p = 0.0010)***	**49.2 (49.2 ± 1.5) (p = 0.0010)***
B: Marian RomCro es-pt	**38.0 (38.0 ± 1.5)**	**61.9 (61.9 ± 1.1)**	**49.2 (49.2 ± 1.5)**
GoogleT es-pt	30.9 (30.9 ± 1.3) (p = 0.0010)*	57.4 (57.4 ± 1.0) (p = 0.0010)*	55.8 (55.8 ± 1.4) (p = 0.0010)*

Table 5: Evaluation results for Spanish-Portuguese

System	BLEU	chrF2	TER
Marian Generic es-ro	18.4	45.4	73.4
Marian RomCro es-ro	**21.4**	48.2	69.5
GoogleT es-ro	20.7	**48.9**	**69.1**

System	BLEU (μ ± 95% CI)	chrF2 (μ ± 95% CI)	TER (μ ± 95% CI)
B: Marian Generic es-ro	18.4 (18.4 ± 1.0)	45.4 (45.4 ± 0.8)	73.4 (73.4 ± 1.3)
Marian RomCro es-ro	**21.4 (21.4 ± 1.0) (p = 0.0010)***	**48.2 (48.2 ± 0.9) (p = 0.0010)***	**69.5 (69.5 ± 1.4) (p = 0.0010)***
B: Marian RomCro es-ro	21.4 (21.4 ± 1.0)	48.2 (48.2 ± 0.9)	69.5 (69.5 ± 1.4)
GoogleT es-ro	20.7 (20.7 ± 1.0) (p = 0.0639)	**48.9 (48.9 ± 0.9) (p = 0.0170)***	69.1 (69.1 ± 1.4) (p = 0.1708)

Table 6: Evaluation results for Spanish-Romanian

improve the quality. We plan to experiment with backtranslation, compiling a monolingual literary corpus for the target language, and machine translate these corpora into the source language to create the backtranslated data. So far the only source language in the experiments is Spanish, and we plan to perform further experiments with the other RomCro languages as source languages.

5 Conclusions and future work

We presented a possible use of RomCro, a multilingual and multidirectional parallel corpus of literary texts in six languages. Our study has illustrated the viability of using the RomCro corpus for training neural machine translation systems specifically designed for literary texts. Notably, our findings indicate that these specialized systems outperform generic models and achieve comparable, if not superior, performance compared to Google Translate.

As for future work, other than experimenting with backtranslation and changing the source language, we plan to enlarge the corpus by adding more literary works and other Romance languages. The main difficulty is the lack of works translated to all the languages in the corpus, and this will be even more difficult if we add more languages.

Appendix A - Metric signatures

- BLEU: nrefs:1 | bs:1000 | seed:12345 | case:mixed | eff:no | tok:13a | smooth:exp | version:2.3.1
- chrF2: nrefs:1 | bs:1000 | seed:12345 |

System	BLEU	chrF2	TER
eval.es-MarianGeneric.hr	13.4	39.0	75.6
eval1K.es-Marian.hr	15.4	41.3	74.6
eval1K.es-GoogleT.hr	**23.6**	**51.2**	**63.7**

System	BLEU (μ ± 95% CI)	chrF2 (μ ± 95% CI)	TER (μ ± 95% CI)
B: Marian Generic es-hr	13.4 (13.4 ± 1.2)	39.0 (39.1 ± 2.2)	75.6 (75.6 ± 2.0)
Marian RomCro es-hr	**15.4 (15.4 ± 1.3) (p = 0.0010)***	**41.3 (41.3 ± 2.3) (p = 0.0010)***	**74.6 (74.6 ± 2.7) (p = 0.1019)**
B: Marian RomCro es-hr	15.4 (15.4 ± 1.3)	41.3 (41.3 ± 2.3)	74.6 (74.6 ± 2.7)
GoogleT es-hr	**23.6 (23.5 ± 1.1) (p = 0.0010)***	**51.2 (51.2 ± 1.1) (p = 0.0010)***	**63.7 (63.7 ± 1.3) (p = 0.0010)***

Table 7: Evaluation results for Spanish-Croatian

case:mixed | eff:yes | nc:6 | nw:0 | space:no | version:2.3.1

- TER: nrefs:1 | bs:1000 | seed:12345 | case:lc | tok:tercom | norm:no | punct:yes | asian:no | version:2.3.1

Acknowledgments

This work was supported by the Croatian Science Foundation under the project number MOBODL-2023-08-9511, funded by the European Union – NextGenerationEU.

References

Akimova, Marina, Anastasia Belousova, Igor Pilshchikov, and Vera Polilova. 2020. Cpcl: A multilingual parallel corpus of poetic texts and new perspectives for comparative literary studies. In *DHN2020: The workshop "Parallel Corpora as Digital Resources and Their Applications"(Riga, 2020): Abstracts*.

Bikić-Carić, Gorana, Bojana Mikelenić, and Metka Bezlaj. 2023. Construcción del romcro, un corpus paralelo multilingüe. *Procesamiento del lenguaje natural*, 70:99–110.

Čermák, Petr. 2019. A parallel corpus of 40 languages. *Parallel Corpora for Contrastive and Translation Studies: New resources and applications*, 90:93.

El-Kishky, Ahmed, Vishrav Chaudhary, Francisco Guzmán, and Philipp Koehn. 2020. Ccaligned: A massive collection of cross-lingual web-document pairs. In *Proceedings of the 2020 Conference on Empirical Methods in Natural Language Processing (EMNLP)*, pages 5960–5969.

Erjavec, Tomaž, Cvetana Krstev, Vladimir Petkevic, Kiril Simov, Marko Tadić, and Duško Vitas. 2003. The multext-east morphosyntactic specification for slavic languages. In *Proceedings of the 2003 EACL Workshop on Morphological Processing of Slavic Languages*, pages 25–32.

Erjavec, Tomaž. 2017. Multext-east. *Handbook of linguistic annotation*, pages 441–462.

Forcada, Mikel L, Mireia Ginestí-Rosell, Jacob Nordfalk, Jim O'Regan, Sergio Ortiz-Rojas, Juan Antonio Pérez-Ortiz, Felipe Sánchez-Martínez, Gema Ramírez-Sánchez, and Francis M Tyers. 2011. Apertium: a free/open-source platform for rule-based machine translation. *Machine translation*, 25:127–144.

Fraisse, Amel, Quoc-Tan Tran, Ronald Jenn, Patrick Paroubek, and Shelley Fisher Fishkin. 2018. Translitex: A parallel corpus of translated literary texts. In *Eleventh international conference on language resources and evaluation (LREC 2018)*. European Language Resources Association (ELRA).

Grabar, Natalia, Olga Kanishcheva, and Thierry Hamon. 2018. Multilingual aligned corpus with ukrainian as the target language. In *SLAVICORP*.

Hansen, Damien and Emmanuelle Esperança-Rodier. 2022. Human-adapted mt for literary texts: Reality or fantasy? In *NeTTT 2022*, pages 178–190.

Junczys-Dowmunt, Marcin, Roman Grundkiewicz, Tomasz Dwojak, Hieu Hoang, Kenneth Heafield, Tom Neckermann, Frank Seide, Ulrich Germann, Alham Fikri Aji, Nikolay Bogoychev, et al. 2018. Marian: Fast neural machine translation in c++. In *Proceedings of ACL 2018, System Demonstrations*, pages 116–121.

Kilgarriff, Adam, Pavel Rychly, Pavel Smrz, and David Tugwell. 2008. The sketch engine. *Practical Lexicography: a reader*, pages 297–306.

Koehn, Philipp, Hieu Hoang, Alexandra Birch, Chris Callison-Burch, Marcello Federico, Nicola Bertoldi, Brooke Cowan, Wade Shen, Christine Moran, Richard Zens, et al. 2007. Moses: Open source toolkit for statistical machine translation. In *Proceedings of the 45th annual meeting of the association for computational linguistics companion volume proceedings of the demo and poster sessions*, pages 177–180. Association for Computational Linguistics.

Koehn, Philipp. 2020. *Neural machine translation.* Cambridge University Press.

Kudo, Taku and John Richardson. 2018. Sentencepiece: A simple and language independent subword tokenizer and detokenizer for neural text processing. In *Proceedings of the 2018 Conference on Empirical Methods in Natural Language Processing: System Demonstrations*, pages 66–71.

Lefer, Marie-Aude. 2021. Parallel corpora. In *A practical handbook of corpus linguistics*, pages 257–282. Springer.

Lefever, Els, Lieve Macken, and Veronique Hoste. 2009. Language-independent bilingual terminology extraction from a multilingual parallel corpus. In *Proceedings of the 12th Conference of the European Chapter of the ACL (EACL 2009)*, pages 496–504.

López Rodríguez, Clara Inés. 2016. Using corpora in scientific and technical translation training: resources to identify conventionality and promote creativity. *Cadernos de traduçao*, 36:88–120.

Oliver, Antoni and Sergi Álvarez. 2023. Filtering and rescoring the ccmatrix corpus for neural machine translation training. In *Proceedings of the 24th Annual Conference of the European Association for Machine Translation*, pages 39–45.

Oliver, Antoni. 2023. Author-tailored neural machine translation systems for literary works. In *Computer-Assisted Literary Translation*, pages 126–141. Routledge.

Padró, Lluís. 2011. Analizadores multilingües en freeling. *Linguamática*, 3(1):13–20.

Papineni, Kishore, Salim Roukos, Todd Ward, and Wei-Jing Zhu. 2002. Bleu: a method for automatic evaluation of machine translation. In *Proceedings of the 40th annual meeting of the Association for Computational Linguistics*, pages 311–318.

Popović, Maja. 2015. chrf: character n-gram f-score for automatic mt evaluation. In *Proceedings of the tenth workshop on statistical machine translation*, pages 392–395.

Post, Matt. 2018. A call for clarity in reporting BLEU scores. In *Proceedings of the Third Conference on Machine Translation: Research Papers*, pages 186–191, Belgium, Brussels, October. Association for Computational Linguistics.

Rei, Ricardo, Craig Stewart, Ana C Farinha, and Alon Lavie. 2020. Comet: A neural framework for mt evaluation. In *Proceedings of the 2020 Conference on Empirical Methods in Natural Language Processing (EMNLP)*, pages 2685–2702.

Reimers, Nils and Iryna Gurevych. 2019. Sentence-bert: Sentence embeddings using siamese bert-networks. In *Proceedings of the 2019 Conference on Empirical Methods in Natural Language Processing.*

Schwenk, Holger, Guillaume Wenzek, Sergey Edunov, Edouard Grave, Armand Joulin, and Angela Fan. 2021. Ccmatrix: Mining billions of high-quality parallel sentences on the web. In *Proceedings of the 59th Annual Meeting of the Association for Computational Linguistics and the 11th International Joint Conference on Natural Language Processing (Volume 1: Long Papers)*. Association for Computational Linguistics.

Sellam, Thibault, Dipanjan Das, and Ankur Parikh. 2020. Bleurt: Learning robust metrics for text generation. In *Proceedings of the 58th Annual Meeting of the Association for Computational Linguistics*, pages 7881–7892.

Snover, Matthew, Bonnie Dorr, Richard Schwartz, Linnea Micciulla, and John Makhoul. 2006. A study of translation edit rate with targeted human annotation. In *Proceedings of the 7th Conference of the Association for Machine Translation in the Americas: Technical Papers*, pages 223–231.

Terzić, Dušica, Saša Marjanović, Dejan Stosic, and Aleksandra Miletic. 2020. Diversification of serbian-french-english-spanish parallel corpus parcolab with spoken language data. In *Text, Speech, and Dialogue: 23rd International Conference, TSD 2020, Brno, Czech Republic, September 8–11, 2020, Proceedings 23*, pages 61–70. Springer.

Tiedemann, Jörg. 2012. Parallel data, tools and interfaces in opus. In *Proceedings of the Eighth International Conference on Language Resources and Evaluation (LREC'12)*, pages 2214–2218.

Toral, Antonio and Andy Way. 2015. Machine-assisted translation of literary text: A case study. *Translation Spaces*, 4(2):240–267.

Varga, Dániel, Péter Halácsy, András Kornai, Viktor Nagy, László Németh, and Viktor Trón. 2005. Parallel corpora for medium density languages. In *RECENT ADVANCES IN NATURAL LANGUAGE PROCESSING*, page 590.

"Can make mistakes": Prompting ChatGPT to Enhance Literary MT output

Gys-Walt van Egdom
Utrecht University
Trans 10, 3512 JK Utrecht, the Netherlands
g.m.w.vanegdom@uu.nl

Onno Kosters
Utrecht University
Trans 10, 3512 JK Utrecht, the Netherlands
o.r.kosters@uu.nl

Christophe Declercq
Utrecht University
Trans 10, 3512 JK Utrecht, the Netherlands
c.j.m.declercq@uu.nl

Abstract

Operating at the intersection of generative artificial intelligence, machine translation, and literary translation, this paper examines to what extent prompt-driven post-editing can enhance the quality of machine-translated literary texts. We assess how different types of instruction influence post-editing performance, particularly focusing on literary nuances and author-specific styles. Situated within posthumanist translation theory, which often challenges traditional notions of human intervention in translation processes, the study explores the practical implementation of generative artificial intelligence in multilingual workflows. While the findings suggest that prompted post-editing can improve translation output to some extent, its effectiveness varies, especially in literary contexts. This highlights the need for a critical review of prompt engineering approaches and emphasizes the importance of further research to navigate the complexities of integrating AI into creative translation workflows effectively.

1 Introduction

Ever since ChatGPT was released in November 2022, the world of language automation for translation purposes – up to that point dominated by neural machine translation (NMT) (Ranathunga 2023) – has entered a new era, the paradigm shifts of which are not yet overly clear. Amid evolving roles of humans and technological processes, the lines between human and non-human translation become increasingly blurred (O'Thomas, 2017). As the need for new theoretical concepts grows, the Huxley family re-emerge (Aldous Huxley's 1932 posthuman *Brave New World* society as well as Julian Huxley's 1957 essay on posthumanism)[1]. Posthumanist theory addresses the expanding human-technology interaction and challenges traditional translation theory by reducing human intervention and pushing human expertise to the periphery of translatorial efforts. Recent advancements in NMT and generative artificial intelligence (GenAI) do indeed offer new methodologies for automating and enhancing multilingual tasks (see Lee 2023 and He 2024). Yet, within that increasing aspiration of translation automation the accurate conveyance of literary works still poses a unique challenge, one that traditional machine translation (MT) systems typically struggle to even remotely approximate (Guerberof-Arenas and Toral 2022; Macken et al. 2022). However, the integration of GenAI tools in the partly, largely or fully automated translation workflow may present a promising avenue for enhancing the quality of MT output in this domain.

At the same time, several questions remain: By combining the precision of machine algorithms with the supposed creativity of Large Language Models (LLMs), can GenAI tools offer a transformative approach to post-editing (PE) neural output? Can

[1] Posthumanist here refers to a collective concept that encompasses various critical theories, all with a shared aim of envisioning a future world that transcends the current material realities defining human existence (see also O'Thomas 2017).

Proceedings of the 1st Workshop on Creative-text Translation and Technology, pages 10–20
June 27, 2024 ©2024 European Association for Machine Translation

prompting mechanisms for GenAI learn from earlier endeavors in automatic post-editing (APE), and vice versa? To what extent can these designs provide for an increase in quality of literary translations that have gone through an automated pipeline? This paper therefore explores the posthumanist intersection of GenAI, MT and literary translation, highlighting both limitations and potential. It aims to reveal how insights from APE can aid GenAI in enhancing already machine translated text and how prompt templates in GPT-4 are an effective means to improve the quality of MT output of literary texts.

2 Related work

APE is utilized to correct MT errors automatically, to enhance the outcomes of MT system, and to reduce human editing work (Vu and Haffari, 2018; Shterionov et al., 2020; Chollampatt et al., 2020). Moreover, APE has become an invaluable methodology when addressing decoder limitations and enabling advanced text analysis beyond typical decoding capabilities (see Bojar et al. 2017).

The practice of adjusting MT output to make sense of nonsensical results has existed since the early days, when MT was also called "mechanical translation" (Bar-Hillel, 1951; Reiffer, 1952). The idea of automating PE tasks, however, remained mostly theoretical for a long period. It remained an idea awaiting the advancement of computing models capable of actualizing the concept (see, for example, Povlsen et al., 1998). This does not exclude ongoing attempts to kickstart an automated pipeline at the back end of MT output. Such a pipeline was needed in situations where initial automated quality estimation would lead to a decision mechanism determining if output should be rejected, accepted for human revision, or assigned to APE in cases of medium MT quality. It should therefore come as no surprise that for years a mature and robust APE application was sought after. Initially grounded in late and hybrid rule-based systems (e.g. Knight and Chander 1994), APE methodologies were designed to fix common mistakes in rule-based MT by capitalizing on the potential of Statistical MT (SMT) techniques. This method proved somewhat effective in addressing consistent errors (see Do Carmo et al. 2021). The proliferation of extensive datasets and the increase in computational power quickly led to a gradual shift towards statistical approaches as state-of-the-art approaches to MT. These SMT models were able to leverage bilingual corpora to identify error patterns and their corrections, signifying a pivotal move toward automation and scalability (ibid.). Within this context, APE was explored to refine SMT output through a two-stage process involving a monolingual translation phase to correct initial translation errors. A wide range of techniques was applied: from maintaining source text (ST) connections for better lexical accuracy to focusing on fluency and correcting data in case of sparsity issues (i.e. a lack of sufficient training examples). Strategies were primarily designed with a view to improving word choice and sentence structure, but they were employed with varying success; SMT models continued to falter in grasping the subtle intricacies of textual and contextual nuances (ibid.).

The concept of APE was central to two EU-funded projects of Belgium-based Crosslang. The Bologna Translation Service (ICT-PSP 270915, March 2011 – February 2013) integrated rule-based and statistical MT with translation memory and automatic and human PE (Depraetere et al. 2011), their APE-Quest (Connecting Europe Facility, project 2017-EU-IA-0151) provided a quality gate by sequencing quality estimation (QE) and APE for medium quality output into the translation workflow of the eTranslation MT system (Depraetere et al. 2020).[2] Towards the end of the 2010s, the concept of APE as a phase in iterative solutions gained attention. APE approaches witnessed a remarkable surge in popularity following their application to so-called "black-box MT systems", such as Neural MT (NMT; see Shterionov et al., 2020; Do Carmo et al. 2021).

NMT ushered in a revolutionary era for APE methodologies. Within this context, techniques have shifted towards leveraging the strengths of neural processing, such as synthetic data training, multiple-source training, and fine-tuning with advanced models like BERT. While the application of APE has diversified, addressing issues like domain adaptation and reduction in retraining needs, the core aim remains to enhance MT output (Vu and Haffari, 2018; Chatterjee 2019; Shterionov et al., 2020; Chollampatt et al., 2020). Neural techniques, particularly those using a transformer architecture, have made significant improvements in grasping context, expressing idiomatic expressions, and identifying more delicate stylistic features. Moreover, employing deep learning techniques, neural APE models seem to offer more coherent and precise corrections, addressing a broader spectrum of errors beyond simple lexical or grammatical errors.

Despite recent advancements in machine translation (MT), challenges persist, largely because neural processing, while significantly improving MT output quality, has introduced greater opacity within the

[2] The APE component for the neural MT output was based on neural copycat networks, itself based on Ive 2019.

processing systems. This "black box" phenomenon makes it difficult to pinpoint the exact locations where errors occur, complicating debugging strategies (Huang et al. 2019; Zhang & Wan 2022). Moreover, there remains an ongoing need for better evaluation metrics that can accurately reflect human judgments of accuracy, fluency and style (Van Egdom et al. 2023; Lyu et al. 2024). These developments and challenges highlight the gap that remains in place between current technological capabilities and the complex requirements of translation.

Amidst these developments in computational linguistics, it is pertinent to highlight that APE, in the traditional sense of the words, is rooted in clear-cut programming paradigms, and no linguists are directly involved in this process – a rather 'posthumanist' endeavor. However, as Generative AI continues to revolutionize the language (technology) industry (see Lyu et al. 2024), radically new forms of APE can be conceived. Novel approaches can seek active engagement of language service providers in supervised editing processes (e.g. 'interactive MT'), and take into account highly context-specific requirements of specific projects (e.g. "stylized translation" and "translation memory based MT"; see Lyu et al. 2024). For instance, this paradigm shift heralds the introduction of 'prompt engineering' within the translation profession (see Raunak et al. 2023). This phenomenon, which gives rise to 'prompted PE', can be considered as a semi-automatic approach to enhancing translation quality. Recent research underscores that the performance of Generative AI can be notably improved through directed instruction, also within the context of translation: in line with the principles of temporary in-context learning, clear and specific prompts are believed to increase the likelihood of obtaining the intended translation output (see Longpre et al. 2023).

3 Materials and Methods

To address the research question about the effectiveness of prompt templates in improving the quality of MT output, a detailed methodological strategy was developed. This strategy aims to assess systematically how structured prompts influence the performance and accuracy of prompted PE results produced by GPT-4.

3.1 Materials

The paper engaged with outputs from a source text previously leveraged in research focusing on MT quality, specifically the work of Van Egdom et al. (2023). In their research project, the output of four MT systems were examined: DeepL, Google Translate, Systran and Sig3Big (the latter being a custom Literary MT engine (CLMT) developed by Toral et al. (2020, 2021)). Over a three-year span, an annual quality evaluation was conducted to assess the development of MT engines, evaluating whether enhancements in self-learning capabilities, data volume, and algorithmic sophistication would yield improved performance over time. In this project, the Sig3Big system was excluded from periodic evaluations. As a result, ten versions derived from the same source text, "I wrote a letter…" by Donald Barthelme (524 words), were analyzed (for a detailed discussion of results, see Van Egdom et al., 2023).

For this present exploratory study, which can be considered an associated spin-off project, new outputs from the systems mentioned above were utilized, along with additional translations from LLMs powered by GPT-3.5 (in ChatGPT, free license), GPT-4 (in ChatGPT, paid license) and Gemini (Bard, free license), all generated in the fall of 2023. The prompt used to generate MT outputs with Generative AI was: "Translate into Dutch". This resulted in a set of seven unedited MT outputs that provided a baseline for the study.

This first step was followed by the generation of three different PE versions of these MT outputs under the following conditions. To generate these versions, ChatGPT was used (GPT-4, paid license). For the first set of revisions ChatGPT was prompted to follow the simple directive "As an expert translation post editor, your task is to post-edit this machine-translated Dutch translation" (condition 1). For the second set (condition 2), the instruction was further refined to draw attention to the original's literary features: "As an expert translation post editor, your task is to post-edit this machine-translated Dutch translation. Pay attention to the literary features in the ST." Under condition 3, target texts were crafted following a more detailed approach: the program was instructed to focus on the unique narrative voice of Donald Barthelme via a scaffolded prompt: Step 1: "Collect information about Donald Barthelme's unique literary style online." Step 2: "Analyze the ST and identify Barthelme's stylistic features in "I wrote a letter…". Use results of online search as a frame of reference." Step 3: "As an expert translation post editor, your task is to post-edit this machine-translated Dutch translation. Pay attention to the literary features in the source text described under step 2". In response to complex assignments (conditions 2 and 3), ChatGPT was asked to explicitly name the steps undertaken, in order to gain insight into (issues with) reasoning. In total, 21 variations were compiled, incorporating both the original text and the unmodified MT outputs within the prompts, to ensure comprehension for the PE tasks at hand. It should be noted that iterations with identical prompts could have led to different outcomes, as each output is considered 'unique'. This variability in output under identical conditions could be said to limit the generalizability of results (Chen et al. 2023).

3.2 Methods

In translation quality assessment, methodologies typically oscillate between holistic and analytical approaches (for an overview of approaches, see Van Egdom et al. 2018). Holistic evaluation tends to view the text as a whole, focusing on the general impression the translated materials leave on the assessor. Analytical methods, on the other hand, tend to dissect the translation minutely, focusing on specific text characteristics, but this goes at the expense of the overall cohesiveness and impact of the text. In our research, an item-specific analytical method, known as the "rich point method", was adopted (for a discussion of the rich point method, see Van Egdom et al. 2018). This approach was designed to pinpoint challenges within the translation task, considering intricacies of the source text (ST), the linguistic gap separating the source and target languages involved, and the explicit information contained in the translation brief.

The selected items, or "rich points", were assessed under three main criteria reflecting critical dimensions of translation quality: accuracy, fluency, and style. These criteria were deemed instrumental in evaluating the general as well as the literary qualities of the outputs, with accuracy and fluency addressing the fundamental correctness and readability of the translation. Over the years, various frameworks for categorizing MT errors have emerged, spanning from broad classifications to more intricate systems like Multidimensional Quality Metrics (MQM) or the SCATE taxonomy. Core to the last are the broad categories of fluency and accuracy, each further divided into separate subcategories (see for instance Fonteyne, Tezcan and Macken 2020). The criterion 'style' addressed the rendering of the literary features of the ST.

The qualitative evaluation of the original MT outputs used to establish a baseline incorporated a meticulously structured analysis based on 28 ST items (see Appendix 1). These elements were deemed crucial for ensuring high-quality output: the list of items consisted of 5 items for accuracy, 7 items for fluency, and 12 items for style. The selection was conducted by two assessors with extensive literary knowledge and near-native proficiency in English and native proficiency in Dutch, in addition to a deep understanding of the relevant cultural contexts. The assessment was conducted by the same assessors, in alignment with the criteria established in the model contract for literary translations in the Netherlands, as outlined by Auteursbond & GAU (2023). Their evaluations classified the solutions into three categories: correct solutions, questionable solutions, and incorrect solutions. Solutions deemed questionable were discussed among the assessors and subsequently reclassified as either correct or incorrect. This classification laid the foundation for a nuanced qualitative analysis of the MT outputs. To ensure robustness and objectivity in the evaluation process, a third assessor, matching the first two in language proficiency and cultural knowledge, was engaged to validate the assessments made by the first assessors (i.e. to ensure inter-rater agreement). This multilayered evaluation methodology aimed to cultivate a comprehensive understanding of target text (TT) quality, grounded in a systematic analysis of text items that reflected key translation challenges in this specific context.

The second phase of the analysis involved a manual assessment conducted by our two assessors. During this phase, the assessors scrutinized the solutions found for the 28 ST items, marked them as either correct, questionable or incorrect, discussed questionable items to ensure dichotomous scoring and then employed a polytomous rating scale, 'neutral' indicating no change in quality; 'positive' denoting improvements; and 'negative' signifying deterioration with regard to the raw output. This evaluation method was designed to capture the nuances of how different instructions influenced the quality of the translated text.

By structuring the analysis in this way, our study aimed to provide a clear overview of how different levels of prompt specificity and instruction can influence the quality of prompted PE outputs. The comparative assessment of raw and PE versions, informed by detailed human evaluation, seeks to offer insights into the practical benefits and limitations of employing advanced AI-driven strategies for enhancing MT output.

4 Results

In the first stage, a detailed qualitative assessment was undertaken to set a standard for translation quality. This encompassed a systematic evaluation of outputs from 7 distinct MT systems. The assessors could award a maximum of 28 points to each text, aligning with the 28 specific items scrutinized during the assessment process. As can be inferred from the results presented in Table 1, the quality of the unedited 'raw MT' outputs appears to be suboptimal, indicating a significant need for thorough post-editing to achieve a level of quality suitable for publication. The aggregate analysis reveals that, on average, the seven systems attained a score of 7, signifying that approximately 25% of the selected source items were accurately translated. In the dataset, two outliers can be identified. The CLMT engine achieves a fairly decent score: nearly 40% of the selected items (11/28) are correctly represented in the TT. In contrast, Systran exhibited the poorest performance, correctly translating only two items, which equates to a mere 7% of the total items. This paper also introduced evaluations of newer systems, including GPT-3.5, GPT-4, Gemini (Bard). Intriguingly, the former two displayed marginally superior performancse compared to established systems like DeepL and Google Translate, while the latter fell behind. Still, it should be noted that, despite optimism vis-à-vis LLM's potential as an MT proxy (Open AI, 2023; Raunak et al. 2023), differences were minimal.

	Accuracy (/5)	Fluency (/7)	Style (/16)	Total (/28)
CLMT 22	2	2	7	**11**
DeepL 23	1	3	3	**7**
Google 23	0	0	7	**7**
Systran 23	0	0	2	**2**
GPT-3.5	0	3	5	**8**
GPT-4	0	1	7	**8**
Gemini	0	1	5	**6**
Sum total raw MT	*3 (/25)*	*10 (/49)*	*36 (/112)*	*49 (/196)*

Table 1. Baseline quality of MT outputs

A positive aspect of itemized evaluation is that it provides insight into the average quality of output, but also reveals that there are various textual aspects where improvements can be observed. For example, when analyzing items concerning 'accuracy' (corresponding to 5 items in total in the ST), only the CLMT (2/5) and DeepL (1/5) systems were noted for correctly rendering items pertinent to this criterion. This shows that the qualitative analysis can be said to serve as a guidepost for targeted improvements, particularly in facets of the translations that directly impact textual accuracy.

Having established a baseline quality for unedited MT output, the study analyzed the impacts of three differentiated editing instructions. Under the first condition, ChatGPT was tasked with comprehensive PE (Full PE) of the MT outputs while considering the source content. Analysis of the data shows a general improvement in translation quality: on average, each text now correctly represents 8.29 items, marking an increase compared to the original MT output (1.29 items more than with the raw MT). Roughly 30% of source items were more accurately rendered, indicating a modest enhancement in overall quality. These results suggest that PE prompting appears to be reasonably effective, and that further specification of prompts could indeed provide additional improvements.

	Accuracy (/5)	Fluency (/7)	Style (/16)	Total (/28)
CLMT 22	1	3	6	**10**
DeepL 23	1	2	5	**7**
Google 23	0	4	3	**7**
Systran 23	1	3	3	**7**
GPT-3.5	0	5	3	**8**
GPT-4	1	3	6	**10**
Gemini	1	3	5	**8**
Sum Total FPE	*5 (/25)*	*23 (/49)*	*31 (/112)*	*57 (/196)*

Table 2. Output quality under condition 1 (FPE)

However, this improvement could also be said to present a complex picture. Notably, the quality enhancement is not uniform across texts: almost half of the FPE texts show quality levels similar to those of the original MT outputs (DeepL, Google, GPT-3.5). Substantial improvements can be primarily attributed to gains in performance observed in the Systran version, which jumped from two to seven correctly resolved items. Gemini and GPT-4 also showed some improvement, enhancing its score by three and two additional items. Conversely, there was one instance of a decrease in quality: after FPE, a correctly resolved item is lost in the CLMT output (score: 10).

The detailed breakdown into subcategories reveals even more nuanced results. While the 'accuracy' category demonstrates room for significant improvement, FPE versions outperform the raw MT results slightly in this respect, increasing from three to five correctly interpreted items in total (5/30). What seems noteworthy is that the CLMT output slightly regressed in terms of accuracy. In contrast, 'fluency' showed a rather marked improvement after FPE, with the number of instances in which fluency-related problems were satisfactorily resolved more than doubling (from ten to twenty-three correct instances after full PE). Despite these gains, a trade-off is observed in the 'style' category, which experienced a serious decline post-FPE. Whereas the raw MT outputs had initially provided satisfactory solutions for style-related items 36 times, this number suddenly dropped to 31 following comprehensive PE. This trend is hardly unexpected, as research on PE guidelines shows that style improvement is rarely explicitly addressed (see Hu & Cadwell 2016). The shifts in output quality for our three subcategories underscore the inherent challenges and compromises involved in balancing the intricate elements of accuracy, fluency, and style in the process of enhancing MT texts with the aid of GenAI technology.

The second condition of the experiment focused specifically on stylistic aspects of the ST, as ChatGPT was tasked with full PE of the outputs while remaining mindful of the literary nuances of the ST. This directive was expected to enhance TT quality by making the instructions more explicit, and, more importantly, tailored to the literary purpose of the text. In theory at least, this instruction would enhance the system's in-context learning performance (Longpre et al. 2023). However, it is not superfluous to add that no specific guidelines were provided regarding the unique literary attributes that were to be preserved or highlighted, thus, leaving ChatGPT to interpret these stylistic nuances autonomously.

	Accuracy (/5)	Fluency (/7)	Style (/16)	Total (/28)
CLMT 22	0	2	5	**7**
DeepL 23	0	3	4	**7**
Google 23	1	1	2	**4**
Systran 23	0	2	2	**4**
GPT-3.5	0	4	6	**10**
GPT-4	0	3	4	**7**
Gemini	1	3	4	**8**
Sum Total FLPE	*2 (/25)*	*18 (/49)*	*27 (/112)*	*47 (/196)*

Table 3. Output quality under condition 2 (Full Literary PE)

As can be inferred from Table 3, preliminary data indicate that the overall quality of the translations does not exhibit the anticipated improvement under these tailored instructions. After implementing a focus on literary features of the original, no fewer than four out of the seven texts experience a decline in performance. On average, under this condition, the translations accurately represent approximately 6.7 out of 28 items, resulting in a meager success rate of 24%. Still, there were a number of exceptions to the rule. Systran, being the odd one out, displays marginal improvement from the base MT output: in the Full LPE version, two additional fluency-related items were rendered successfully (from two to four correct items). Similarly, the GPT-3.5 and Gemini versions show a slight uptick when it comes to performance, with enhancement observed under both fluency and style for GPT-3.5 and accuracy and fluency for Gemini.

Still, the overarching trend points to a diminution in quality. This decrease becomes even more pronounced when analyzing the remaining versions. An already limited success in conveying accuracy seen in previous conditions further regresses, with almost all items (2 in total) being misrepresented under condition 2. The odd exceptions are observed in the Google version and the Gemini version: each version managed to capture one single item for accuracy. Moreover, contrary to expectations, the 'style' category, the primary focus of this condition, witnesses a substantial downturn: initially, the raw outputs collectively presented 36 correct solutions, yet, under condition 2, this tally decreases to 27. It can be safely assumed that this reduction stems from GPT's unique interpretation of 'literariness', which seems to stray from the traditional (highly intricate) balance between form and content found in literary style, instead veering towards a more embellished, often overwrought rendition. This interpretation tends to produce what can be considered a 'pastiche' version of the ST rather than a faithful literary rendition. GPT, rather than representing the literary style specific to the ST, applies lexical choices it presumably understands as 'literary'. In doing so, it shows its inability to source beyond the overwhelming amount of stylistically unremarkable (clichéd, hackneyed) non-literary understandings of literature it can find. Nevertheless, a rather interesting observation emerges in the category 'fluency', where the literary tone of voice appears to foster fluency: this is evidenced by an increase from ten to eighteen correct translation solutions. This suggests that while attempts to infuse a literary style clearly compromises accuracy and literary authenticity, the unintentional result is an improvement in the overall fluency displayed in the texts.

In an attempt to refine the approach to stylistic fidelity, the third condition of the experiment was construed around an even more structured and detailed prompt. The prompt was divided into three stages, providing a scaffolded approach. The task involved: 1) collecting online information about Donald Barthelme's unique literary style; 2) analyzing the ST to identify Barthelme's stylistic elements in "I wrote a letter..."; and 3) utilizing this understanding during the PE process to maintain the original literary qualities (typical of Barthelme's writing) in the subsequent versions. This third instruction was aimed at guiding ChatGPT towards a deeper engagement with the literary characteristics of the ST, moving beyond a highly superficial interpretation of 'literariness'.

Surprisingly, the results presented in Table 4 show that this intensified focus led to a mere 15.3% of items being accurately resolved across the board. The Systran and the Gemini versions were the sole versions demonstrating any improvement under these author-specific directives. Gemini showed a rise to six correctly represented items (raw MT score: 2). With seven accurately rendered items, Gemini performed marginally better under the author-specific condition (raw MT score: 6). The remaining systems failed to solve more than four items correctly, suggesting a broad decline in performance.

	Accuracy (/5)	Fluency (/7)	Style (/16)	Total (/28)
CLMT 22	0	3	1	**4**
DeepL 23	1	1	2	**4**
Google 23	0	1	2	**3**
Systran 23	0	3	5	**8**
GPT-3.5	0	1	1	**2**
GPT-4	0	1	1	**2**
Bard (Gemini)	1	3	3	**7**
Sum Total Tailored LPE	2 (/25)	13 (/49)	15 (/112)	**30 (/196)**

Table 4. Output quality under condition 3 (Tailored Literary PE)

The breakdown of results further underscores the challenges introduced by the author-tailored instruction. Unlike the previous conditions, where some degree of improvement was noted in at least one category (accuracy under FPE, fluency under FLPE), precise and clear instruction with a focus on Barthelme's literary style had a detrimental effect on performance in all categories. Again, this decline can be attributed to several factors. Firstly, a noticeable increase in omissions can be found in the target output, with ChatGPT tending to exclude significant portions of the text (mostly toward the end of the text), resulting in a blatant loss of content, as well as a distortion and simplification of Barthelme's short story. Similar issues are observed in other studies focusing on LLMs, particularly in chain-of-thought settings (e.g. Raunak et al. 2023). LLM's are prone to not only omitting key elements but also inventing non-existent off-target content or twisting the existing information in incomprehensible ways. This phenomenon, referred to as 'edit hallucinations', compounds the distortion and simplification observed in Barthelme's short story. Furthermore, our tailored approach seemed to encourage an over-the-top form of pastiche – a kind of pastiche of the pastiche – transitioning from a general literary imitation to an unsatisfactory mimicry of Barthelme's literary style. Particularly, the nuanced balance between the mundane and the absurd that is characteristic of Barthelme's story is completely lost on GPT. In the latest iterations, this stark imbalance manifested in versions that simply veer towards the grotesque, stripping away the subtlety and nuanced banality, the hallmarks of Barthelme's narrative style. This misinterpretation, particularly evident in hyperbolic renditions of the texts, highlights the difficulties in capturing the intricate interplay of tones and themes inherent to Barthelme's oeuvre using LLMs.

5 Discussion

The findings from this study clearly reflect the challenges of prompt engineering as a means to optimize MT output through PE instructions. Reflecting on the improvement brought about by FPE, it becomes evident that while prompted PE can indeed enhance translation output – a finding that is consistent with observations made in Raunak 2023 et al. – its effectiveness seems limited and is markedly inconsistent. The experiment's venture into more tailored instructions, under the condition 'Full Literary PE' , brought to light the complexities of encoding stylistic nuances in language models. The decline observed in output quality under this condition prompts a critical reassessment of approaches to 'literariness' in Transformer architectures. The third condition's attempt to incorporate author-specific nuances into PE widened the divide separating algorithmic interpretation from literary sensibility even further.

The nuanced implications of these findings beckon a reevaluation of our expectations from prompt engineering and language models, particularly within the context of MT output optimization. Both within and beyond the academic realm, there is significant emphasis on the importance of prompt engineering and the refinement of prompts and prompt templates. While it is acknowledged that LLMs display unpredictable responses to similar prompts, there seems to be a need for precise and refined prompts and templates (see Longpre et al. 2023; Lyu et al. 2024). However, it appears that refinement, particularly in the form of instructions tailored to a literary context, currently leads to weaker output. This issue is primarily due to the tendency to beautify texts, a tendency associated within translation theoy with Berman's "ennoblement" or "popularization" (1985). The question now is whether this tendency can be suppressed through radically different or more refined instruction or specific settings (e.g. system instructions as provided through custom GPT's).

6 Conclusion

The project detailed in this paper is situated at the intersection of on the one hand posthumanist translation theory, which in itself reconsiders notions of human intervention in translation, and the practical application of GenAI in multilingual workflows on the other. With this project, we have sought to explore the potential of prompted PE, a form of semi-automatic PE, as a substitute for human PE or an intermediary step to refine MT outputs and add an additional step to translation automation in workflows. Our exploratory study scrutinized seven MT versions of a literary short story through the PE process, revealing that prompted PE, under specific conditions, yields marginal improvements. It was striking that more specific instructions, targeted toward literary translations, led to weaker performances. This outcome was quite intriguing as the view is widely held that prompt specificity is a driver of performance in AI-driven tasks, such as language translation (Longpre et al. 2023).

Still, it is crucial to acknowledge the preliminary nature of these findings. As with much research in the nascent field of Generative AI and translation, our study faces limitations that underscore a great need for further exploration. From a fundamental point of view, different takes on 'literariness' and 'style' can be applied to measure the creative prowess of GenAI (see Boase-Beier 2020). For a more comprehensive understanding of the 'literariness' of PE outputs, future research should also include a greater variety of literary genres and styles. Additionally, there is a great need to expand research on the effects of prompted PE across a broader spectrum of languages (as in Lyu et al. 2024). Finally, adverse effects of prompted PE might be mitigated when using different prompting strategies than the ones used in this study. To counteract observed 'pastiche effect', example-based prompts, laying down clear criteria for the tone and the expected levels of faithfulness to the original, can be explored. Another avenue for future research in the domain of literary translation is investigating the effects of customizing GPT's using domain-specific language resources such as translation memories (see Zhang and Wan 2022).

Recent advancements in language automation have illuminated the potential of AI integration into linguistic workflows, not in the least in creative text domains. However, amidst the hype surrounding GenAI, the intrinsic complexity of creative tasks (e.g. literary translation) often gets overlooked or oversimplified in research in computational linguistics and translation studies. Despite the critical acclaim for AI's creativity and the benefits of human-language prompting, our research has shown that it is and will always remain crucial to ensure a tight alignment between creativity and fidelity in the context of creative translation.

References

Bar-Hillel, Y. 1951. The Present State Of Research On Mechanical Translation. In *American Documentation*, 2(4): 229-237.

Barthelme, Donald. 1992. I wrote a letter… In *The Teachings of Don B.* (pp. 11-12). Berkeley : Counterpoint.

Berman, A. 1985. La traduction et la lettre ou l'auberge du lointain. In *Les Tours de Babel* (pp. 31-85). Mauvezin: Trans-Europ-Repress.

Boase-Beier, J. 2020. *Translation and Style* (2nd edition). London : Routledge.

Bojar, O., Chatterjee, R., Federmann, C., Graham, Y., Haddow, B., Huang, S., Huck, M., Koehn, P., Liu, Q., Logacheva, V., Monz, C., Negri, M., Post, M., Rubino, R., Specia, L., & Turchi, M. 2017. Findings of the 2017 conference on machine translation (WMT17). *In Proceedings of the Second Conference on Machine Translation*, pages 169–214. Copenhagen, Denmark: Association for Computational Linguistics.

Chen, B., Zhang, Z., Langrené, N, & Zhu, S. 2023. Unleashing the potential of prompt engineering in large language models: a comprehensive review. ArXiv: https://arxiv.org/pdf/2310.14735

Chatterjee, R., Federmann, C., Negri, M., & Turchi, M. 2019. Findings of the WMT 2019 shared task on automatic post-editing. In P*roceedings of the Fourth Conference on Machine Translation* (Volume 3: Shared Task Papers, Day 2), pages 11–28. Florence, Italy: Association for Computational Linguistics.

Chollampatt, S., Susanto, R. H., Tan, L., & Szymanska, E. 2020. Can automatic post-editing improve NMT? In Proceedings of the 2020 Conference on Empirical Methods in Natural Language Processing (EMNLP), pages 2736–2746. Online: Association for Computational Linguistics.

Do Carmo, F., Shterionov, D., Moorkens, J., et al. 2021. A review of the state-of-the-art in automatic post-editing. *Machine Translation*, 35: 101–143. https://doi.org/10.1007/s10590-020-09252-y

Depraetere, H., Van den Bogaert, J., & Van de Walle, J. 2011. Bologna translation service: Online translation of course syllabi and study programmes in English. In *Proceedings of the 15th Annual Conference of the European Association for Machine Translation*, pages 29-34. Leuven, Belgium, May.

Depraetere, H., Van Den Bogaert, J., Szoc, S., & Vanallemeersch, T. 2020. APE-QUEST: An MT quality gate. In *Proceedings of the 22nd Annual Conference of the European Association for Machine Translation*, pages 473-474.

Do Carmo, F., Shterionov, D., Moorkens, J., et al. 2021. A review of the state-of-the-art in automatic post-editing. *Machine Translation*, 35: 101–143.

Fonteyne, M., Tezcan, A., & Macken, L. 2020. Literary machine translation under the magnifying glass: Assessing the quality of an NMT-translated detective novel on document level. In *12th International Conference on Language Resources and Evaluation (LREC). European Language Resources Association (ELRA)*, pages 3783-3791.

Guerberof-Arenas, A., & Toral, A. 2022. Creativity in translation: Machine translation as a constraint for literary texts. *Translation Spaces,* 11(2): 184-212.

He, S., 2024. Prompting ChatGPT for Translation: A Comparative Analysis of Translation Brief and Persona Prompts. *arXiv preprint* arXiv:2403.00127.

Hu, K., & Cadwell, P. 2016. A comparative study of post-editing guidelines. In *Proceedings of the 19th Annual Conference of the European Association for Machine Translation*, pages 34206–353.

Huang, X., Liu, Y., Luan, H., Xu, J., & Sun, M. 2019. Learning to copy for automatic post-editing. In Proceedings of the 2019 Conference on Empirical Methods in Natural Language Processing and the 9th International Joint Conference on Natural Language Processing (EMNLP-IJCNLP), pages 6122–6132. Hong Kong, China: Association for Computational Linguistics.

Huxley, A. 1932. *Brave New World.* London: Chatto and Windus.

Huxley, J. 1957. Transhumanism. In *New Bottles in New Wine*, London: Chatto and Windus, pages 13-18. https://archive.org/details/NewBottlesForNew-Wine/page/n7/mode/2up

Ive, J., Madhyastha, P. S., & Specia, L. 2019. Deep copycat networks for text-to-text generation. In *Proceedings of the 2019 Conference on Empirical Methods in Natural Language Processing and the 9th International Joint Conference on Natural Language Processing (EMNLP-IJCNLP)*, pages 3227-3236.

Knight, K., & Chander, I. 1994. Automated postediting of documents. In Proceedings of the 12th National Conference on Artificial Intelligence (AAAI 1994), Vol. 1: 779–784. Seattle, Washington, USA.

Lee, T.K., 2023. Artificial intelligence and posthumanist translation: ChatGPT versus the translator. *Applied Linguistics Review*, https://doi.org/10.1515/applirev-2023-0122.

Longpre, S., Hou, L., Vu, T., Webson, A., Chung, H. W., Tay, Y., Zhou, D., Le, Q. V., Zoph, B., Wei, J., & Roberts, A. 2023. The Flan Collection: Designing data and methods for effective instruction tuning. arXiv. https://arxiv.org/abs/2301.13688

Lyu, C., Du, Z., Xu, J., Duan, Y., Wu, M., Lynn, T., Aji, A. F., Wong, D. F., Liu, S., & Wang, L. 2024. A paradigm shift: The future of machine translation lies with large language models. arXiv. https://arxiv.org/abs/2305.01181

Macken, L., Vanroy, B., Desmet, L., & Tezcan, A. 2022. Literary translation as a three-stage process: Machine translation, post-editing and revision. In *23rd Annual Conference of the European Association for Machine Translation. European Association for Machine Translation*, pages 101-110.

Naveed, H., Khan, A. U., Qiu, S., Saqib, M., Anwar, S., Usman, M., Barnes, N., & Mian, A. S. 2023. A Comprehensive Overview of Large Language Models. ArXiv, abs/2307.06435. Retrieved from https://api.semanticscholar.org/CorpusID:259847443

O'Thomas, M. (2017). Humanum ex machina: Translation in the post-global, posthuman world. *Target* 29(2): 284-300.

Povlsen, C., Underwood, N. L., Music, B., & Neville, J. 1998. Evaluating text-types suitability for Machine Translation: a case study on an english-danish MT System. In *LREC*, pages *27-34.*

Ranathunga, S., Lee, E. S. A., Prifti Skenduli, M., Shekhar, R., Alam, M., & Kaur, R. 2023. Neural machine translation for low-resource languages: A survey. *ACM Computing Surveys, 55(11): 1-37.*

Raunak, V., Sharaf, A., Wang, Y., Awadalla, H., & Menezes, A. 2023. Leveraging GPT-4 for Automatic Translation Post-Editing. In Findings of the Association for Computational Linguistics: EMNLP 2023, pages 12009–12024. Singapore: Association for Computational Linguistics.

Reifler, E. 1952. Mechanical translation with a pre-editor, and writing for MT. In *Proceedings of the Conference on Mechanical Translation.*

Shterionov, D., Do Carmo, F., Wagner, J., Hossari, M., Paquin, E., & Moorkens, J. 2020. A roadmap to neural automatic post-editing - an empirical approach. *Machine Translation*, 34: 67–96.

Shterionov, D., Wagner, J., & Do Carmo, F. 2019. APE through neural and statistical MT with augmented data. ADAPT/DCU submission to the WMT 2019 APE shared task. In *Proceedings of the Fourth Conference on Machine Translation (WMT2019), Volume 3: Shared Task Papers*, pages 132–138. Florence, Italy.

Van Egdom, G.W., Verplaetse, H., Schrijver, I., Kockaert, H., Segers, W., Pauwels, J., Bloemen, H. & Wylin, B. (2018). How to put the translation test to the test? On preselected items evaluation and perturbation. In *Quality Assurance and Assessment Practices in Translation and Interpreting* (pp. 26-56). Hershey [MA]: IGI Global.

Van Egdom, G.W., Kosters, O., & Declercq, C. 2023. The Riddle of (Literary) Machine Translation Quality: Assessing Automated Quality Evaluation Metrics in a Literary Context. *Revista Tradumàtica*, 21: 129–159.

Vu, T.-T., & Haffari, G. 2018. Automatic post-editing of machine translation: A neural programmer-interpreter approach. In *Proceedings of the 2018 Conference on Empirical Methods in Natural Language Processing,* pages 3048–3053. Brussels, Belgium: Association for Computational Linguistics.

Zhang, X., & Wan, X. 2022. An empirical study of automatic post-editing. arXiv. https://arxiv.org/abs/2209.07759

Appendix 1. Source text items and corresponding analytical criteria

	Item	Criterion
1	, asked him	Style - colloquialism
2	towaway zones	Accuracy
3	and I didn't like it	Fluency
4	Cost me …, plus	Style - colloquialism
5	tiny little cars	Style - colloquialism
6	You ever notice …? You ever seen…? No you haven't.	Style - colloquialism [Fluency]
7	, and to keep some mental health warm …,	Style - colloquialism [Fluency]
8	a bucket of ribs	Accuracy
9	Which I would gladly carry up there…	Fluency - idiom
10	I cabled him	Style - absurdism [Accuracy]
11	and, by the way, what was the apartment situation up there?	Style - colloquialism [Fluency]
12	It was bad,	Fluency - idiom
13	he replied by platitudinum plate	Style - absurdism [Accuracy]
14	but what could he do?	Fluency - idiom
15	root cellar	Accuracy
16	'cause of me being a friend of the moon.	Style - colloquialism
17	pretty nice place	Fluency
18	the Space Shuttle Hurry-Up Fund	Accuracy
19	Drumming fiercely on a hollow log with a longitudinal slit tuned to moon frequencies	Style - absurdism [Accuracy]
20	employment, medical coverage, retirement benefits, tax shelterage, convenience cards, and Christmas Club accounts	Accuracy
21	That's a roger,	Fluency - idiom
22	he moonbeamed back	Style- absurdism [Accuracy]
23	by means of curly little ALGOL circuits I had knitted myself on my Apple computer	Style(absurdism), [Accuracy]
24	that ticktacktoe was about as far as they'd got in that direction	Style - absurdism [Accuracy]
25	via flights of angels with special instructions	Style – absurdism [Accuracy]
26	it looked to me like he had things pretty well in hand up there	Fluency
27	Part-time if need be?	Style – colloquialism
28	a shower of used-car asteroids with blue-and-green bumper stickers	Style – absurdism [Accuracy]

LitPC: A set of tools for building parallel corpora from literary works

Antoni Oliver
Universitat Oberta de Catalunya (UOC)
aoliverg@uoc.edu

Sergi Álvarez
Universitat Oberta de Catalunya (UOC)
salvarezvid@uoc.edu

Abstract

In this paper, we describe the LitPC toolkit, a variety of tools and methods designed for the quick and effective creation of parallel corpora derived from literary works. This toolkit can be a useful resource due to the scarcity of curated parallel texts for this domain. We also feature a case study describing the creation of a Russian-English parallel corpus based on the literary works by Leo Tolstoy. Furthermore, an augmented version of this corpus is used to both train and assess neural machine translation systems specifically adapted to the author's style.

1 Introduction

A parallel corpus is a collection of texts, each of which is translated into one or more other languages than the original. Parallel corpora are invaluable resources for researchers and professionals in the fields of literary studies, contrastive linguistics, machine translation, and literary translation. While there are many parallel corpora which can be accessed and checked online, the Opus Corpora[1] (Tiedemann, 2009) stands out as a primary collection. However, the representation of literary texts within these corpora is often limited. Opus Corpora lists few corpora for the literary domain and each corpus includes a limited number of parallel segments. Table 1 includes an overview of the total number of parallel segments in the Opus Corpora compared with the parallel segments for the literary domain, across three highly-resourced language pairs. The scarcity of resources in this domain means that researchers in literary studies, scholars in machine translation, and professional literary translators who seek to integrate parallel corpora for literary texts into their daily work must compile their own parallel corpora.

In this paper, we introduce different resources, software, and methodologies for the rapid and effective generation of parallel corpora from literary texts. While the programs and methodologies outlined are applicable across various subjects, the section dedicated to resources focuses specifically on literary texts.

Language Pair	All	Literature
eng-rus	185 M	17.6 K
eng-spa	922 M	97.1 K
eng-fra	787 M	0.1 M

Table 1: Parallel segments in Opus Corpora: total and literature corpora.

2 Sources for literary works

When compiling a literary corpus, the first thing we should consider is the copyright status of the original works and their translations. Copyright laws safeguard the rights of authors and translators for a specified duration-—typically ranging from 70 to 100 years, varying by country, after the death of the author or translator. Upon expiration of this term, the works enter into the public domain. Numerous online sources offer literary works for download; however, many such sources operate illegally, granting unauthorized access to copyrighted texts. To lawfully acquire copyrighted material, one must meticulously examine the copyright laws pertinent to each country. This process

[1]https://opus.nlpl.eu/

Proceedings of the 1st Workshop on Creative-text Translation and Technology, pages 21–31
June 27, 2024 ©2024 European Association for Machine Translation

often entails negotiations with the rights holders. It's noteworthy that in certain jurisdictions, purchasing a book may confer the right to utilize its content for non-commercial use, although this provision is not universally assured by all legal frameworks.

In this section, we explore various avenues for legally obtaining literary works that have entered the public domain, thereby ensuring unrestricted access and usage rights for any intended purpose.

To effectively develop machine translation (MT) systems focused on the literary domain, it is essential to create both parallel and monolingual corpora derived from literary texts with the language combinations involved in our project. There is a vast array of books which can be accessed online. Once found, they need to be downloaded, transformed into text format, and subsequently processed to generate the desired corpus. The following sources are particularly noteworthy:

- Project Gutenberg[2]
- Wikisource[3]
- Feedbooks[4]
- Hathi Trust Digital Library[5]
- Archive.org
- Standard Ebooks[6]

For our case study, we need to obtain the works by Leo Tolstoy in Russian and English. First of all, we use a website which is very popular for its extensive collection of Russian classical literature: Библиотека Максима Мошкова[7]. While it is ambiguous whether the site exclusively hosts public domain works, it is certain that Leo Tolstoy's contributions have been in the public domain for some time, as he passed away in 1910.

Additionally, to obtain the English translation, we use Project Gutenberg. This website offers a searchable database, complemented by daily updated catalog files. The LitPC toolkit encompasses a utility that interprets these catalogs in RDF format, enabling the search for books based on criteria such as author, title, language, the author's lifespan, and subject matter. These parameters can be specified as either strings or regular expressions, and searches can combine multiple criteria. Utilizing this functionality, the tool displays a curated list of works that align with the specified search parameters. Users have the flexibility to refine their search or modify the list of works. Upon finalization, the tool facilitates the download of the selected works in epub format to a designated directory.

3 Basic processing steps

3.1 Conversion to text

After downloading all the works in the different language combinations, we need to process them. To do so, we need them in text format and in Unicode UTF-8 encoding. This process can be performed with any external tool, but for convenience, the LitPC toolkit provides a program capable of converting all epub files in a given directory to text. It can either place all the converted files in a given directory or produce a text file with all the contents of all epub files in the directory.

3.2 Segmentation

After conversion to text, the next step is text segmentation. This process divides the text into segments, which are usually sentences. This task can be performed by analyzing the periods that can be found in the text. A set of rules indicates whether each of the periods are splitting points. These rules are defined using regular expressions and are typically expressed using a standard XML format called Segmentation Rules eXchange (SRX). The toolkit includes a program that can use SRX files to segment a single file or all the files included in a directory. In the toolkit, different SRX files are included for different languages, even though other SRX files can also be used.

If no SRX file is available for a given language, we can use a trainable segmenter implemented in the NLTK library (Bird, 2006). This segmenter uses the algorithm created by Kiss and Strunk (2006) and can be trained on a large unsegmented corpus of a given language. The same corpus to be segmented can be used for training. Once trained, the segmenter can be customised using a list of abbreviations for the language. The LitPC toolkit also implements a program for training and customizing a segmenter and a program for segmenting using the trained model.

[2] https://www.gutenberg.org/
[3] https://wikisource.org/
[4] https://www.feedbooks.com/catalog/public_domain
[5] https://www.hathitrust.org/
[6] https://standardebooks.org/
[7] http://lib.ru/

Both available segmenters can optionally add the paragraph mark (<p>) to the segmented text. As we will see in the next section, this mark can be useful for one of the automatic alignment strategies.

4 Automatic text alignment

After the basic pre-processing steps, we will have segmented text that we want to align. The segmented text can either include two text files or two directories–one for each language–containing the segmented text files.

There are several freely available automatic text alignment strategies. In the LitPC toolkit we use two different algorithms: one based on more classical techniques (which assumes parallel documents), and another one based on sentence embeddings (which is able to find translated segment pairs even in non-parallel texts).

As we are working with original literary works and its translations, it would seem clear that these are parallel documents for which we can seamlessly apply parallel document techniques. However, there are some elements which can turn a published original work into semi-parallel or comparable documents. Some of these factors include:

- The translated work is not from the same edition as the original work. In these cases, the changes are usually very small and can be handled by parallel document techniques. In other cases, however, the changes are significant. For example, a collection of some short stories is translated, but the translated published book changes the order of the short stories. In such cases, techniques for comparable corpora are appropriate.

- Either the original or the translation, or both, contain introductions, prefaces or other elements that make it impossible to align the document using classical techniques. The amount of human work required to manually edit the documents to make them equal is very important, so it is more efficient to use alignment techniques for comparable corpora. In the case of documents obtained from Project Gutenberg, they include a large section explaining the licence and terms of use.

- When bulk aligning documents, they must have the same name and be placed in two directories, or they must use the same name plus a suffix indicating the language of the document. This means spending additional time renaming all the files. To save time, in such cases we can align all the content in each language without taking into account the document information. This can be done with techniques for comparable documents.

4.1 From parallel documents

If we have two parallel documents or two directories, one containing a set of documents in a source language and the other containing the translated documents, we can use well-known techniques for document alignment. When working with a large number of documents in two directories, the relationship between the source and target documents must be easily deduced from their names. To facilitate this task, the source and target documents should have the same name, or only differ in the suffixes that indicate the language of the documents.

One of the most widely used automatic document alignment programs is Hunalign[8] (Varga et al., 2007). To achieve better results with this programme, we can:

- Include the paragraph mark (<p>) when segmenting the files.

- Use a bilingual dictionary for the language pair. The programme requires a bilingual dictionary to perform the alignment. Even though it is not mandatory and an empty file can be used, using bilingual dictionaries improves performance. Bilingual dictionaries are text files with one entry per line which follows the format *target word @ source word*, as in the following example for a English-Spanish alignment dictionary:

  ```
  hogar @ home
  ```

The toolkit provides Python scripts to create alignment dictionaries from the transfer dictionaries of the Apertium machine translation system (Forcada et al., 2011) and from MUSE[9] (*Multilingual Unsupervised and Supervised Embeddings*) (Conneau et al., 2017).

[8]https://github.com/danielvarga/hunalign

[9]https://github.com/facebookresearch/MUSE

4.2 From comparable documents

It is possible to find translated segments in a large collection of multilingual documents, even though they are not exact translated versions. If we can have a representation of each sentence in a document, we can then compare it to the representations which appear in another language to find the most similar one. If two sentences have sufficiently similar representations, we can infer that they are translation equivalents.

We can represent the sentences with sentence embeddings using a multilingual model. Then, calculating the cosine distance between all the sentences in the source language and in the target language, we can find those sentence pairs having the smaller distance. If this distance is small enough, we can select this sentence pair as translation equivalent. We have adapted an algorithm that can be found in the SBERT website, following the ideas of Artetxe and Schwenk (2019). The full process can be divided into the following steps:

- Representing all sentences in the source and target corpus by their sentence embeddings using a multilingual model. By default, as recommended by Reimers and Gurevych (2020), we use the LaBSE model (*Language-agnostic BERT Sentence Embeddings*) (Feng et al., 2022). To implement the algorithm, we use the Sentence-Transformers library[10], and LaBSE is integrated into the library. Any other model can be used with the provided algorithm.
- For each sentence in the source corpus, using its sentence embedding representation, the algorithm finds the k nearest neighbor sentences in the target corpus. Typical choices for k are between 4 and 16. The cosine distance between the embedding representations is used as a measure.
- All possible source-target sentence combinations are scored using a measure. Instead of directly using the cosine distance, a margin criterion is used, where the cosine distance for all the k nearest neighbors in both directions is considered, as explained by Artetxe and Schwenk (2019).
- The pairs with the highest margin scores are the most likely translated sentences. After the alignment, a visual inspection is required to set a minimum value and discard all pairs below that threshold. Usually, scores higher than 1.2 or 1.3 work very well.

This algorithm is implemented in the LitPC toolkit and can be used with or without a GPU unit.

5 Cleaning of parallel corpora

When obtaining an available parallel corpus or compiling our own corpus, we can find several common errors. Hence, it is always advisable to clean the corpus. The toolkit distributes a cleaning script that can perform, among others, the following cleaning operations:

- Apostrophe normalization: replacing the typographic apostrophe with the standard one.
- Removing HTML and XML tags.
- Replacing HTML/XML entities with their respective characters.
- Removing segment pairs where one is empty.
- Removing segments pairs where one or both are shorter than a given threshold.
- Removing segment pairs with equal segments.
- Removing segment pairs with a percent of numeric characters higher than a given threshold.
- We can set a file containing a set of strings. If a segment pair contains any of these strings, it will be removed.
- Removing segment pairs matching a set of regular expressions stated in a given file.
- Checking the source and target languages.
- Remove segments pairs with one or both segments written in upper case.
- Fixing encoding errors.

The Python langid library, which is able to detect 97 languages, is used to detect the language. However, the precision of language detection is relatively low for short text segments in a parallel corpus. Thus, a set of languages expected in the corpus can be given to increase the performance of the algorithm.

[10] https://www.sbert.net/

5.1 Rescoring of parallel corpora

Once cleaned, we have a corpus that does not include any of the aforementioned problems. To ensure these segment pairs are translation equivalents, we can calculate a score that provides a measure of the translation equivalence between the source and target segments in the segment pair. It can be achieved using sentence embeddings. We can encode the source and target segments in the segment pairs with sentence embeddings using a multilingual model, as explained in Section 4.2. The cosine distance between the source and target embeddings can be used as a score.

The toolkit provides a program that performs two actions:

- Language detection of the source and target segments, using fasttext[11] (Bojanowski et al., 2016). This tool offers two interesting features: it returns the detected language along with a detection confidence score and users can easily train their own language detection models.
- Scoring of all the segments with the cosine distance of the sentence embedding representation calculated using a multilingual model (LaBSE by default).

After the scoring process is completed, we provide a companion program used to select the parallel segments which match the language and the language detection confidence score. A minimum confidence score is required based on the cosine distance.

6 Enlarging the corpus using general language parallel corpora

In our use case, we utilize the compiled parallel corpus to train a neural machine translation system. Most likely, the compiled corpus will not be large enough to train an NMT system. Millions of parallel segments are required for a successful training. Preliminary experiments have shown that a good starting point would be 5 million segments, even though 10 or 15 million would be a better threshold.

In case there is a very large parallel corpus available for the required language pair, we can automatically select from the large general corpus the segments which are more similar to the ones found in the domain corpus. The procedure is very similar to the described in Moore and Lewis (2010). Let us call corpus A the small in-domain corpus (in our case, the parallel corpus from Tolstoy's works) and corpus B the very large general corpus. This process involves the following steps.

Fist of all, a language model is calculated from the source language part of corpus A. The perplexity of all source segments of corpus B is calculated using the language model. Then, all source and target segments of corpus B along with perplexity are stored in a database.

Once the calculations are finished, we select a given number of segments from the database, sorting them according to the perplexity in ascending order. This whole process can be performed using a program available in the LitPC toolkit.

7 Use case: Russian-English NMT model tailored to Tolstoy works

As an experimental part, we compiled a Russian-English parallel corpus from the works of Lev Nikolayevich Tolstoy, a Russian writer who was born in 1828 and died in 1919.

7.1 Original works and translations

We downloaded the original works and its translation into English in fb2 and epub format and converted them into text with Python scripts available in the LitPC toolkit.

We downloaded a total of 42 original works in Russian from Библиотека Максима Мошкова. We also downloaded all the English translations of Tolstoy's works available in Project Gutenberg.

The complete list of works used to create the corpus can be found in Appendix A. Please note that the list of original works is different from that of translated works.

After converting the files into text, they were segmented. For each language, all the segments of all the works were concatenated, and repeated segments were eliminated. As a result, we obtained a file containing all the unique Russian segments (a total of 118,755 segments) and a file containing all the unique English segments (a total of 200.013 segments).

7.2 Alignment

We used the alignment strategy for comparable corpora to align the two files containing unique segments in Russian and English. We can see these

[11] https://fasttext.cc/

two files as a comparable or semi-parallel corpus, as there is no line-by-line relationship between the two files. We obtained a file containing 74,998 aligned pairs. Each pair contains information on the margin score assigned to this pair. The file is sorted in descending order by the margin score; therefore, the first segments are more likely to be correctly aligned. In Table 2, we can observe some examples of alignments with higher scores (and correctly aligned) and with lower scores (incorrectly aligned).

7.3 Available Russian-English corpora

To build a large Russian corpus, we used a series of parallel corpora available in Opus Corpora. However, we must keep in mind that in the available corpora, we usually do not have information about the source and target languages. Any language in the pair can be the source, and both segments can be translated from another language. The following parallel corpora were used: CCMatrix, CCAligned, Wikimatrix, Paracrawl, and UNPC.

- **CCMatrix** (Schwenk et al., 2021b) is a parallel corpus extracted from web crawls. Each web document is converted to text, the language is identified and then segmented. All the segments in a given language are treated together, without having into account the document where it comes from, so the document information is not used. To create the parallel corpus from language A to language B, all segments in A are compared with all segments in B. The comparison is performed after converting the segments into sentence embeddings using a multilingual model. In this way, sentences in language A are very close in the multidimensional space to sentences in language B with similar meanings. Using the cosine distance, a margin score is calculated as explained in Artetxe and Schwenk (2019) to detect segment pairs with a high chance to be mutual translations.

- **CCAligned** is a parallel corpus compiled in a very similar manner as CCMatrix. In this case, though, document information is used. Only segments in the documents detected as parallel are aligned. The alignment is also performed using sentence embeddings. The process of creation of this corpus is described in El-Kishky et al. (2020).

- **Wikimatrix**: To compile this corpus (Schwenk et al., 2021a), Wikipedia articles in 85 languages were used. Authors don't limit the process to alignments with English and all possible language pairs are considered. It is very important to keep in mind that Wikipedia articles in different languages are different documents, and only eventually some articles or sections of articles are translations from other language versions. However, as the same articles in different languages explain the same concepts, it's likely to find segments being translation equivalents, even when the articles are written independently. To detect equivalent segments, similar techniques to the ones used in CCMatrix and CCAligned are used.

- **Paracrawl** (Bañón et al., 2020): A corpus developed within an EU-project that also provides tools for crawling the web in the search of parallel documents to be aligned. Initially, it only included EU languages, but more languages are being added, including the English-Russian pair.

- **UNPC**: The United Nations Parallel Corpus (Ziemski et al., 2016) was created from manually translated documents of the United Nations from 25 years (1990 to 2014). It is available in six official languages at the UN: Arabic, Chinese, English, French, Russian, and Spanish. All the alignments have been performed using Hunalign (Varga et al., 2007). The corpus does not contain information about the source language, but most of the original documents at UN are written in English or French. This is not a general corpus, but we have included it because it is a high-quality corpus.

7.4 Preprocessing of the available corpora

Before creating the corpus from the available corpora, we carried out several preprocessing steps:

- Elimination of repeated segments, using the standard Linux commands cat, sort, uniq and shuf.

- Cleaning of the corpora using the program described in section 5. The following cleaning operations have been performed:
  - Apostrophe normalization.

Source segment	Target segment	Margin score
Неприступная Мальта сдается без выстрела; самые неосторожные распоряжения увенчиваются успехом.	Impregnable Malta surrenders without a shot; his most reckless schemes are crowned with success.	1.6393
Берегись делать какое-нибудь различие, могущее нарушить равенство.	Beware of making any distinctions which may infringe equality.	1.6101
...	...	...
Запил, так запил!	When I drink, it's there!	1.0000
Скверность это, значит, не по закону это.	It's filthy, that's what I call it; it's not right.	1.0000

Table 2: Examples of obtained parallel segments from the Tolstoy's works and translations (the two segments with the highest and the lowest margin scores are presented)

- Removing of HMT/XML tags
- Removing of control characters
- Unescaping of HTML/XML entities
- Fixing encoding errors
- Removing segment pairs with one side empty
- Removing segments pairs with one part or both shorter than 10 characters
- Removing segment pairs with more thant 60% of numerical expression characters
- Removing segments pairs with equal source and target

Table 3 shows the size of the individual and final corpus after these operations.

Corpus	Size (segments)
CCMatrix	139,863,720
CCAligned	13,341,868
Wikimatrix	1,617,622
Paracrawl	5,318,501
UNPC	28,581,489
TOTAL	**178,686,030**

Table 3: Size of the Russian-English parallel corpora available in Opus Corpora used in the experiments

7.5 Rescoring of the corpora

Both the corpus from Tolstoy's works and the large corpus created from existing corpora were rescored using the tool described in Section 5.1. This rescoring process re-verifies the languages and computes a distance between the sentence embeddings of the source and target segments, using SBERT. The language detection model is able to return the language code together with a confidence score. In our experiments, we use a language detection threshold of 0.75 for both languages. This figure has been set after experimenting with several values and observing a good compromise between the final number of segments and the quality of the alignment. In Table 4 we can see the number of segments obtained after filtering out the segment pairs with a SBERT score lower than the indicated for the Tolstoy's parallel corpus. Table 5 shows the values for the large parallel corpus.

SBERT score	Segments
0.9	5,336
0.8	34,270
0.75	46,571
0.7	55,209
0.6	65,365
0.5	69,521
no filtering	74,998

Table 4: Size of the Tolstoy corpus with different minimum values of SBERT scores

7.6 Corpus combination

The size of Tolstoy corpus, regardless of the minimum SBERT score, and even without any filtering

SBERT score	Segments
0.9	31,899,731
0.8	116,247,528
0.75	135,595,366
0.7	145,935,126
0.6	154,980,096
0.5	158,014,261
no filtering	178,686,030

Table 5: Size of the large general corpus with different minimum values of SBERT scores

at all, is clearly insufficient to train an NMT system. In order to obtain a larger corpus, we used the corpus combination program described in Section 6. We have used the version filtered with a minimum value of SBERT score of 0.75. We have created three corpora in this way by selecting 10M, 20M and 30M parallel segments from the large corpus. Furthermore, we obtained three subcorpora for each size of the selected corpus:

- A training corpus using the selected segments from the large corpus and a fragment of the Tolstoy corpus (the remaining segments after the creation of the validation and evaluation corpus).
- A validation corpus using 5,000 segments from the Tolstoy corpus.
- An evaluation corpus using 5,000 segments from the Tolstoy corpus

As the parallel corpora have been deduplicated, no common segments are present in the three subsets. Table 6 shows the size of all the corpora:

	Segments		
Train	10,036,571	20,036,571	30,036,571
Val	5,000	5,000	5,000
Eval	5,000	5,000	5,000

Table 6: Size of the corpora used for training the NMT systems

7.7 Training of the NMT systems

The following NMT systems have been trained:

- A system using the large general corpus with a rescoring with a minimum SBERT score of 0.9 (Marian Gen.).
- A system using the corpus resulting from the combination of the Tolstoy corpus with 10M segments selected from the rescored general corpus (Marian 10M).
- A system using the corpus resulting from the combination of the Tolstoy corpus with 20M segments selected from the rescored general corpus (Marian 20M).
- A system using the corpus resulting from the combination of the Tolstoy corpus with 30M segments selected from the rescored general corpus (Marian 30M).

All the corpora were preprocessed using SentencePiece (Kudo and Richardson, 2018) with the following parameters: joining languages: False; model type: bpe; vocabulary size 64,000; vocabulary threshold: 50. The (sub)word alignments of the training corpus were computed calculated using eflomal (Östling and Tiedemann, 2016) in order to use guided-alignment in the training.

The NMT system was trained using the Marian-nmt toolkit (Junczys-Dowmunt et al., 2018) with a transformer configuration. Two validation metrics were used: bleu-detok and cross-entropy. The early-stopping criterion was set to 5 on any of the metrics, and the validation frequency was set to 5,000.

7.8 Evaluation of the trained systems

We have evaluated all the trained systems and compared them with an open neural translation model (OpusMT[12]), that will be considered as the baseline, and two widely used commercial systems: Google Translate[13] and DeepL[14]. To evaluate the systems we used three automatic metrics implemented in Sacrebleu[15] (Post, 2018): BLEU, chrF2 and TER. Appendix B shows the signatures of the three metrics stating the exact configuration parameters as reported by Sacrebleu.

Table 7 shows the evaluation results. In the evaluation, paired bootstrap resampling test with 1,000 resampling trials have been performed, using the -paired-bs option in Sacrebleu. In this way, each system is pairwise compared to the baseline system OpusMT. Assuming a significance threshold

[12] https://github.com/Helsinki-NLP/OPUS-MT-train/tree/master/models/ru-en
[13] https://translate.google.com/
[14] https://www.deepl.com
[15] https://github.com/mjpost/sacrebleu

System	BLEU ($\mu \pm 95\%$ CI)	chrF2 ($\mu \pm 95\%$ CI)	TER ($\mu \pm 95\%$ CI)
Baseline: OpusMT	17.8 (17.8 ± 1.0)	42.4 (42.4 ± 0.8)	68.8 (68.8 ± 1.2)
MarianGen.en	16.0 (16.0 ± 0.8) (p = 0.0010)*	40.8 (40.8 ± 0.7) (p = 0.0010)*	70.0 (70.0 ± 1.1) (p = 0.0060)*
Marian 10M	18.7 (18.7 ± 0.9) (p = 0.0240)*	42.2 (42.2 ± 0.8) (p = 0.1688)	67.6 (67.6 ± 1.1) (p = 0.0200)*
Marian 20M	19.2 (19.2 ± 0.8) (p = 0.0020)*	43.7 (43.7 ± 0.7) (p = 0.0010)*	67.2 (67.2 ± 1.0) (p = 0.0020)*
Marian 30M	19.1 (19.1 ± 0.8) (p = 0.0040)*	43.2 (43.2 ± 0.7) (p = 0.0120)*	67.7 (67.7 ± 1.1) (p = 0.0150)*
GoogleT.en	25.6 (25.6 ± 1.0) (p = 0.0010)*	50.3 (50.3 ± 0.8) (p = 0.0010)*	61.6 (61.6 ± 1.2) (p = 0.0010)*
DeepL	24.9 (24.9 ± 1.1) (p = 0.0010)*	49.7 (49.7 ± 0.8) (p = 0.0010)*	63.1 (63.1 ± 1.3) (p = 0.0010)*

Table 7: Evaluation results for the NMT systems

of 0.05, the null hypothesis can be rejected for p-values < 0.05 (marked with "*" in the tables.)

Regarding the BLEU score, all systems except the Marian Generic get better results than Opus MT. Even the Marian 10M improves compared the baseline system for this metric. In fact, almost all tailored Marian systems are obtaining better results than the baseline OpusMT for all metrics. The only exception is chrF2 score for Marian 10M, that obtains slightly lower results than the baseline, but falling to pass the significance test.

This leads us to conclude that the author-tailoring methodology outlined in this paper can be highly productive. This assertion is further supported by comparing the evaluation metrics of all the tailored systems with those of the Marian Generic systems, which were trained using the same parameters as the tailored systems.

Nevertheless, it's important to acknowledge that both the baseline system and all the trained systems achieve evaluation scores which are lower to those of commercial systems. This suggests that there is still room for improvement, both in the selection of general and literature-specific corpora, as well as in improving the training processes. Anyway, it's important to note that the training sets of the commercial systems may include segments in our evaluation set and this could lead to over-optimistic evaluations.

8 Conclusions and future work

In this paper, we introduce LitPC, a toolkit designed for swiftly generating parallel corpora from literary texts. These versatile tools can also be applied to create parallel corpora for various other subjects. All tools are made available under a free license (GNU-GPL v.3) and can be downloaded from GitHub[16].

We have additionally showcased an experiment involving the development of author-tailored Russian-English NMT systems for Tolstoy's works. The evaluation demonstrates the efficacy of the proposed methodology, although there remains potential for further enhancements to attain results comparable to those of the examined commercial systems. In future experiments we plan to fine-tune exiting models instead of training from scratch and comparing the two strategies.

The future work is planned in two directions: to experiment with fine tuning existing NMT models for literature; and to explore the use of parallel corpora aligned in larger units than segments, as paragraphs or chapters, as suggested by Voigt and Jurafsky (2012).

References

Artetxe, Mikel and Holger Schwenk. 2019. Massively multilingual sentence embeddings for zero-shot cross-lingual transfer and beyond. *Transac-*

[16] `https://github.com/aoliverg/litpc`

tions of the association for computational linguistics, 7:597–610.

Bañón, Marta, Pinzhen Chen, Barry Haddow, Kenneth Heafield, Hieu Hoang, Miquel Esplà-Gomis, Mikel L Forcada, Amir Kamran, Faheem Kirefu, Philipp Koehn, et al. 2020. Paracrawl: Web-scale acquisition of parallel corpora. In *Proceedings of the 58th Annual Meeting of the Association for Computational Linguistics*, pages 4555–4567.

Bird, Steven. 2006. Nltk: the natural language toolkit. In *Proceedings of the COLING/ACL 2006 Interactive Presentation Sessions*, pages 69–72.

Bojanowski, Piotr, Edouard Grave, Armand Joulin, and Tomas Mikolov. 2016. Enriching word vectors with subword information. *arXiv preprint arXiv:1607.04606*.

Conneau, Alexis, Guillaume Lample, Marc'Aurelio Ranzato, Ludovic Denoyer, and Hervé Jégou. 2017. Word translation without parallel data. *arXiv preprint arXiv:1710.04087*.

Feng, Fangxiaoyu, Yinfei Yang, Daniel Cer, Naveen Arivazhagan, and Wei Wang. 2022. Language-agnostic bert sentence embedding. In *Proceedings of the 60th Annual Meeting of the Association for Computational Linguistics (Volume 1: Long Papers)*, pages 878–891.

Forcada, Mikel L, Mireia Ginestí-Rosell, Jacob Nordfalk, Jim O'Regan, Sergio Ortiz-Rojas, Juan Antonio Pérez-Ortiz, Felipe Sánchez-Martínez, Gema Ramírez-Sánchez, and Francis M Tyers. 2011. Apertium: a free/open-source platform for rule-based machine translation. *Machine translation*, 25:127–144.

Junczys-Dowmunt, Marcin, Roman Grundkiewicz, Tomasz Dwojak, Hieu Hoang, Kenneth Heafield, Tom Neckermann, Frank Seide, Ulrich Germann, Alham Fikri Aji, Nikolay Bogoychev, et al. 2018. Marian: Fast neural machine translation in c++. In *Proceedings of ACL 2018, System Demonstrations*, pages 116–121.

Kiss, Tibor and Jan Strunk. 2006. Unsupervised multilingual sentence boundary detection. *Computational linguistics*, 32(4):485–525.

Moore, Robert C and William Lewis. 2010. Intelligent selection of language model training data. In *Proceedings of the ACL 2010 conference short papers*, pages 220–224.

Östling, Robert and Jörg Tiedemann. 2016. Efficient word alignment with markov chain monte carlo. *The Prague Bulletin of Mathematical Linguistics*, (106):125–146.

Post, Matt. 2018. A call for clarity in reporting BLEU scores. In *Proceedings of the Third Conference on Machine Translation: Research Papers*, pages 186–191, Belgium, Brussels, October. Association for Computational Linguistics.

Reimers, Nils and Iryna Gurevych. 2020. Making monolingual sentence embeddings multilingual using knowledge distillation. In *Proceedings of the 2020 Conference on Empirical Methods in Natural Language Processing (EMNLP)*, pages 4512–4525.

Schwenk, Holger, Vishrav Chaudhary, Shuo Sun, Hongyu Gong, and Francisco Guzmán. 2021a. Wikimatrix: Mining 135m parallel sentences in 1620 language pairs from wikipedia. In *Proceedings of the 16th Conference of the European Chapter of the Association for Computational Linguistics: Main Volume*, pages 1351–1361.

Schwenk, Holger, Guillaume Wenzek, Sergey Edunov, Édouard Grave, Armand Joulin, and Angela Fan. 2021b. Ccmatrix: Mining billions of high-quality parallel sentences on the web. In *Proceedings of the 59th Annual Meeting of the Association for Computational Linguistics and the 11th International Joint Conference on Natural Language Processing (Volume 1: Long Papers)*, pages 6490–6500.

Tiedemann, Jörg, 2009. *News from OPUS - A Collection of Multilingual Parallel Corpora with Tools and Interfaces*, volume V, pages 237–248.

Varga, Dániel, Péter Halácsy, András Kornai, Viktor Nagy, László Németh, and Viktor Trón. 2007. Parallel corpora for medium density languages. In *Recent Advances in Natural Language Processing IV*, pages 247–258. John Benjamins.

Voigt, Rob and Dan Jurafsky. 2012. Towards a literary machine translation: The role of referential cohesion. In *Proceedings of the NAACL-HLT 2012 Workshop on Computational Linguistics for Literature*, pages 18–25.

Ziemski, Michał, Marcin Junczys-Dowmunt, and Bruno Pouliquen. 2016. The united nations parallel corpus v1. 0. In *Proceedings of the Tenth International Conference on Language Resources and Evaluation (LREC'16)*, pages 3530–3534.

Appendix A. List of Tolstoy's works and translations

Original Tolstoy's works:

Детство; Отрочество; Юность; Семейное счастье; Война и мир; Анна Каренина; Воскресение; Два гусара; Альберт; Поликушка; Холстомер; Смерть Ивана Ильича; Дьявол; Казаки; Набег; Рубка леса; Записки маркёра; Утро помещика; Метель; Разжалованный; Три смерти; Крейцерова соната; Отец Сергий; Хаджи-Мурат; Севастополь в декабре месяце; Севастополь в мае Севастополь в августе 1855 года; Хозяин и работник; Алеша Горшок; Ягоды; Корней Васильев; Отец Сергий (варианты); Сказки; Декабристы; Первый винокур, Власть тьмы;

Записки сумасшедшего; Божеское и человеческое

English translations:

A Letter to a Hindu; Anna Karenina; A Russian Proprietor, and Other Stories; Bethink Yourselves!"; Boyhood; Childhood; Fables for Children, Stories for Children, Natural Science Stories, Popular Education, Decembrists, Moral Tales; Father Sergius; Fruits of Culture; Katia; Master and Man; My Religion; On the Significance of Science and Art; Plays: Complete Edition, Including the Posthumous Plays; Redemption and two other plays; Resurrection; Sebastopol; Sevastopol; The Awakening (The Resurrection); The Cause of it All; The Census; in Moscow; The Cossacks: A Tale of 1852; The Devil; The First Distiller; The Forged Coupon, and Other Stories; The Invaders, and Other; Stories; The Journal of Leo Tolstoi (First Volume—1895-1899); The Kingdom of God is Within You Christianity and Patriotism Miscellanies; The Kingdom of God Is Within You" Christianity Not as a Mystic Religion but as a New Theory of Life; The Kingdom of God is Within You; What is Art?; The Kreutzer Sonata and Other Stories; The Light Shines in Darkness; The Live Corpse; The Power of Darkness; Three Days in the Village, and Other Sketches. Written from September 1909 to July 1910.; Tolstoi for the young: Select tales from Tolstoi; Tolstoy on Shakespeare: A Critical Essay on Shakespeare; War and Peace, Book 01: 1805; War and Peace; What Is Art?; What Men Live By, and Other Tales; What Shall We Do?; What to Do? Thoughts Evoked by the Census of Moscow; What to Do? Thoughts Evoked By the Census of Moscow; Where Love is There God is Also; Youth;

Apendix B. Metric signatures

- BLEU nrefs:1 | bs:1000 | seed:12345 | case:mixed | eff:no | tok:13a | smooth:exp | version:2.3.1
- chrF2 nrefs:1 | bs:1000 | seed:12345 | case:mixed | eff:yes | nc:6 | nw:0 | space:no | version:2.3.1
- TER nrefs:1 | bs:1000 | seed:12345 | case:lc | tok:tercom | norm:no | punct:yes | asian:no | version:2.3.1

Prompting Large Language Models for Idiomatic Translation

Antonio Castaldo
University of Naples L'Orientale, Italy
University of Pisa, Italy
antonio.castaldo@phd.unipi.it

Johanna Monti
University of Naples L'Orientale, Italy
jmonti@unior.it

Abstract

Large Language Models (LLMs) have demonstrated impressive performance in translating content across different languages and genres. Yet, their potential in the creative aspects of machine translation has not been fully explored. In this paper, we seek to identify the strengths and weaknesses inherent in different LLMs when applied to one of the most prominent features of creative works: the translation of idiomatic expressions. We present an overview of their performance in the EN→IT language pair, a context characterized by an evident lack of bilingual data tailored for idiomatic translation. Lastly, we investigate the impact of prompt design on the quality of machine translation, drawing on recent findings which indicate a substantial variation in the performance of LLMs depending on the prompts utilized.

1 Introduction

Recent advancements in the field of artificial intelligence, particularly with the emergence of Generative Pre-trained Transformer (GPT) models, have prompted the beginning of a new era of exploration into the applicability of large language models (LLMs) for machine translation tasks. The recent development and refinement of LLMs, such as GPT-3.5 and GPT-4 (Brown et al., 2020), have demonstrated their remarkable performance in understanding and generating natural language (Ahuja et al., 2023), thus positioning these models at the forefront of research into the translation of creative textual genres, including the nuanced task of translating idiomatic expressions. Traditional neural machine translation (NMT) systems often falter in accurately capturing the essence of idiomatic expressions, tending towards translations that are either overly literal or misinterpret the intended meaning. In contrast, recent studies have illustrated the ability of GPT models to adopt less literal translation approaches, especially in handling idiomatic expressions, leveraging an enhanced understanding of context and figurative language. This contribution will evaluate various large language models (LLMs) to establish benchmarks for their effectiveness in translating idiomatic expressions in the English-Italian language pair. The objective is to identify the strengths and weaknesses inherent in different LLMs when applied to machine translation (MT) tasks, particularly focusing on the nuanced aspect of creative language. Furthermore, the study will explore the impact of prompt design on MT quality, drawing on the findings of Ahuja et al. (2023) that suggest that the performance of LLMs in multilingual tasks can vary significantly with the prompts used. Through these evaluations, we seek to contribute to the improvement of machine translation technologies, highlighting the potential of LLMs to make creative works more accessible across languages, enriching cultural exchange and overcoming language barriers.

2 Related Work

Research in the use of large language models for machine translation has been pursued following two main axes. The first involves issues specific to LLMs, such as the influence that prompt templates

Proceedings of the 1st Workshop on Creative-text Translation and Technology, pages 32–39
June 27, 2024 ©2024 European Association for Machine Translation

may have on the model output (Zhang et al., 2023; Lu et al., 2023; Peng et al., 2023). The second line focuses on the evaluations of LLMs in various translation scenarios, covering multilingual (Jiao et al., 2023b; Hendy et al., 2023; Zhu et al., 2023), document-level (Wang et al., 2023; Karpinska and Iyyer, 2023; Wu et al., 2024), low-resource translation (Moslem et al., 2023a; Mao and Yu, 2024), hallucination (Guerreiro et al., 2023) and domain adaptation (Hendy et al., 2023). This study positions itself within the second research axis, concentrating on the evaluation of LLMs in specialized translation scenarios. Despite the large body of research currently being conducted on LLMs performance, research to date has not yet fully explored their application to the translation of creative texts. This study does not aim to provide a comprehensive overview of the topic, but we seek to evaluate the intricate task of translating idiomatic expressions, a critical aspect that challenges the adaptability and understanding of these models.

3 Experimental Setup

In this section, we describe the methodology used in our experiments, including the translation process and the evaluation metrics employed. We initiated the translation process leveraging OpenAI API and the HuggingFace library (Wolf et al., 2020) in Python, generating four batches of translations using four distinct prompts applied to the models `gpt-3.5-turbo` and `Mistral-7B-v0.1`.

For the machine translation (MT) evaluation, we used the online evaluation platform MATEO (Vanroy et al., 2023), which provides an easy-to-use user interface for the evaluation of translations, utilizing state-of-the-art neural and n-gram evaluation metrics. We conducted the experiment in three independent trials to ensure the reliability of the results and replicability of the experiment.

3.1 Dataset Selection

In this section, we describe the composition of the dataset used for our experiments, which comprises a set of 350 Italian-English sentence pairs, where 18 idiomatic expressions are used in both their literal and idiomatic meanings. This corpus was assembled utilizing two primary sources: the Italian Dodiom corpus (Eryiğit et al., 2023) and the Reverso Context online database. The Dodiom corpus, a curated collection of Italian and Turkish idiomatic expressions, was initially gathered using a gamified crowdsourcing bot on the Telegram platform. After being collected, the corpus underwent a rigorous annotation process by linguistic experts, as detailed in Morza et al. (2022). The revision process ensured the idioms' authenticity and their contextual relevance.

Leveraging the idiomatic expressions collected using the Dodiom corpus, we proceeded to extract corresponding bilingual sentence pairs that incorporate these idioms from the Reverso Context database. Reverso Context, known for its extensive repository of real-life language usage examples across multiple languages, served as an ideal resource for obtaining authentic usage examples of the idiomatic expressions we have collected.

3.2 Annotation

The 321 extracted sentence pairs were thoroughly evaluated and annotated. This step was crucial to verify the translation accuracy of the idioms and to confirm their relevance within the given contexts, regardless of the initial quality level of Reverso Context. The annotation process was conducted by a native Italian speaker, who had completed a Master's degree in linguistics, accumulating five years of academic education. Their linguistic proficiency and compatibility with our study is certified by English, being the primary language of their university studies. The annotation was conducted on an online platform, developed in Flask, specifically for the scope of this study.

First, the annotator was asked to conduct a binary evaluation of the adequacy of each pair of bilingual sentences, focusing on whether the translated expressions conveyed the original meaning and nuance of the idiom in the source language, and whether the translation extracted by Reverso Context was relevant to the source text. This step allowed us to exclude incorrect and irrelevant examples. Then, the annotator was asked to annotate whether the idiomatic expressions within each sentence were used in their literal or figurative sense. Finally, before beginning our experiments, we proceeded to remove every sentence pair considered unsatisfactory in their translation and relevance.

The process allowed us to obtain a curated dataset, comprised of 254 bilingual segments, on which we could conduct an evaluation of MT quality and prompting impact.

3.3 Prompt Templates

For our study, we select four prompt templates, three of which are derived from studies by Gao et al. (2024), Zhang et al. (2023), and Jiao et al. (2023b), and a five-shot prompt, developed within the scope of our current study. The prompts were chosen on the basis of the high performance reported in the relative literature. The prompt templates that we have selected differ in their length and in the information they convey to the model.

We present an overview of the prompt templates in the following table, with the following annotations: ♦ shows the presence of a line break, `[src]` stands for source language, `[tgt]` stands for target language, and `[input]` stands for the text to be translated.

Prompt ID	Prompt Template
A	[src]: [input] ♦ [tgt]:
B	Please provide the [tgt] translation for this sentence: [input] ♦ Translation:
C	This is a [src] to [tgt] translation, please provide the [tgt] translation for this sentence: [input] ♦ Translation:
D	[src]: [source$_1$] ♦ [tgt]: [target$_1$] ♦ ... [src]: [source$_k$] ♦ [tgt]: [target$_k$] ♦ [src]: [input] ♦ [tgt]:

Table 1: Overview of the prompt templates used in this study

Prompt A offers a concise structure that directly maps the source language to the target language, where brevity is exchanged for clarity of the instructions, which in this case is inferred from the context. Prompt B presents a more descriptive approach, including the target language in a clear instruction, however the source language is not included. Prompt C is the most descriptive one, presenting detailed instructions that include both the source and the target language.

Our contribution, Prompt D, extends the concept of minimalistic mapping (as in Prompt A) through a few-shot learning approach. It involves presenting the model with five contextual examples ($k = 5$) prior to the translation task, selected for their relevance to the input text. This methodology is designed to leverage the model's in-context learning ability (Brown et al., 2020) to improve the translation performance thanks to the exposure to related translation examples (Garcia et al., 2023; Lu et al., 2023). For the implementation of this five-shot prompt, the examples were selected on the basis of their semantic similarity to the input sentence. Whereas the common procedure is to generate semantic embeddings with models such as LaBSE (Hendy et al., 2023), we provide a proof of concept using a computationally efficient and non-neural TF-IDF Vectorizer. Despite its simplicity, the vectorizer effectively represents the texts in a multidimensional space, allowing the calculation of cosine similarity to identify examples most relevant to the given input sentence. This strategy aims to provide the model with contextually pertinent examples, thereby enhancing its ability to infer and execute the translation task.

4 Evaluation

We present a comprehensive evaluation of the four prompt templates we have selected, using two models: `gpt-3.5-turbo-1106` and `Mistral-7B-v-0.1`. Our evaluation used two mainstream neural evaluation metrics: COMET (Rei et al., 2020) and BLEURT (Sellam et al., 2020). These metrics have shown a very high correlation with human judgment and are established in the evaluation of LLM-based machine translation (Moslem et al., 2023a; Hendy et al., 2023). We have decided to include BLEU (Papineni et al., 2002) in our evaluation, as it remains a widely recognized standard metric in MT evaluation, despite its limitations for our specific translation context. More specifically, in the context of accurately conveying idiomatic expressions into another language, there is frequently a mismatch between the length of the sentence in the source and target texts. Metrics such as BLEU and ChrF (Popović, 2015) may not be the most adequate for the task, as they tend to penalize length, lexical discrepancies and brevity of the translations, which are not necessarily indicative of poor translation quality, especially in the context of idiomatic expressions.

4.1 Results with GPT-3.5

When testing the model `gpt-3.5-turbo`, the five-shot template we developed, Prompt D, consistently outperformed the others in terms of BLEURT and COMET scores, displaying statistical significance (p-value < 0.05) in every evaluation instance, as shown in Table 2. Prompt C was the second best-performing prompt in BLEURT and COMET, and the absolute best in terms of BLEU score.

Table 2: Evaluation of automated MT metrics for the selected prompts, using the model gpt-3.5-turbo-1106. Asterisks represent statistical significance (p-value < 0.05).

System	BLEURT	COMET	BLEU
Prompt A	70.09	80.78	36.39
Prompt B	70.17	81.05	37.43
Prompt C	70.54*	81.16*	**38.25***
Prompt D (k=5)	**71.17***	**81.71***	37.70*

The observed BLEU scores were found to be significantly unsatisfactory, in line with expectations. Interestingly, this shortfall cannot be attributed to a discrepancy in sentence lengths, which were quite similar to both the source text (with an average sentence length of 16.98) and the reference translations (with an average sentence length of 17.95). Instead, the limitations may stem from the brevity penalty inherent in the BLEU metric, coupled with a lack of n-gram overlap in the translations.

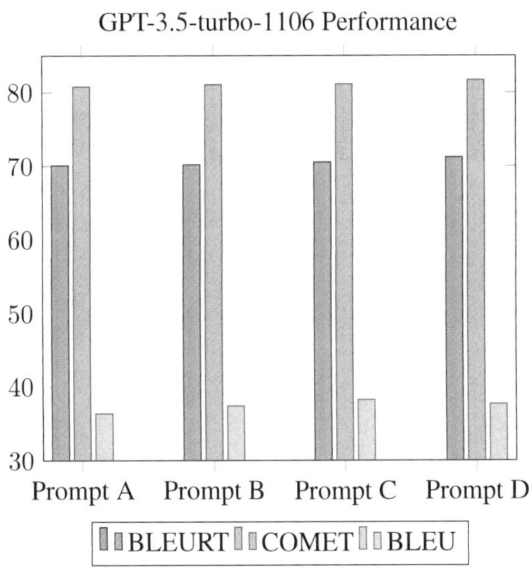

Figure 1: GPT-3.5-turbo-1106 performance per prompt template, calculated by BLEU, COMET and BLEURT.

This issue is particularly pronounced in the handling of idiomatic expressions, where translations often adopt a more creative and less order-bound approach. This hypothesis is supported by a substantial difference in the average BLEU scores: sentences with idiomatic meanings scored an average of 32, while sentences with literal meanings achieved an average score of 39.7. This discrepancy is significantly less pronounced when evaluated using the COMET metric, which shows only a 3-point difference between the two scenarios. In contrast, neural metrics consistently yielded high scores, surpassing 70 across all tested prompts. This suggests that while traditional metrics like BLEU may struggle to evaluate the nuances of creative translations, particularly of idiomatic expressions, neural-based evaluation metrics such as COMET offer a more effective assessment, potentially capturing aspects of translation quality that BLEU overlooks, thanks to their use of semantic embeddings.

4.2 Results with Mistral-7B

The second model we evaluated is the open-source multilingual LLM, `Mistral-7B` (Jiang et al., 2023), developed by the homonymous French company. As reported in the release publication, Mistral has excelled on several NLP benchmarks. Remarkably, its smallest checkpoint, trained on only 7B parameters, has outperformed much larger models, such as `LLama-2-13B` and `LLama-1-34B`, developed by Meta. When fine-tuned on a downstream machine translation task, Mistral has outperformed `gpt-3.5-turbo`, as seen in Moslem et al. (2023b), demonstrating the capability of Mistral to be an effective open source asset for multilingual machine translation.

Table 3: Evaluation of automated MT metrics for the selected prompts, using the model Mistral-7B-v0.1. Asterisks represent statistical significance (p-value < 0.05).

System	BLEURT	COMET	BLEU
Prompt A	64.85	76.55	33.84
Prompt B	64.21	75.76*	32.91
Prompt C	64.98	76.78	33.11
Prompt D (k=5)	**68.60***	**79.56***	**36.57***

Upon testing Mistral on the same set of prompt templates from our preceding experiment, it was observed that Mistral's adherence to given instructions was not as precise as the model developed by OpenAI. Prompt A and C were the worst performing templates, whereas the more informative Prompt C scored better than the others. Even in this case, five-shot prompting (Prompt D) displayed the best results in every evaluation instance.

The translations generated by Mistral were found to include numerous unnecessary excerpts and hallucinations. The core issue identified was not the quality of the translation per se, but the format of the responses. These did not align with the expected format derived from the reference and the source texts. Instead, Mistral introduced extraneous phrases like "Perhaps, you would..." or "I think an accurate translation would be..." which inevitably led to lower scores on evaluative metrics, especially n-gram based ones (Table 3 and Figure 2).

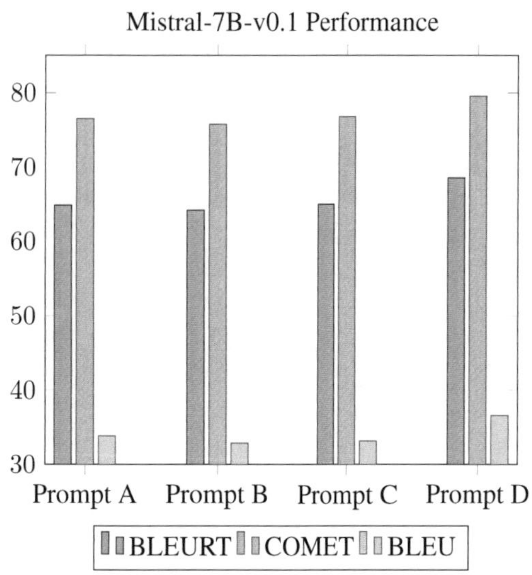

Figure 2: Mistral-7b-v0.1 presents very low BLEU scores for Prompts B and C.

Contrary to previous expectations, our findings reveal that a single machine translation prompt can indeed deliver optimal performance across both ChatGPT and Mistral-7B models. This challenges the conventional wisdom that prompts need to be meticulously customized for each model to elicit the best output. Our analysis suggests that the shared architecture and similar training datasets of these models might allow them to understand and process instructions in a comparable manner, thus offering similarly effective performance to the same prompt. The successful application of one prompt across these models highlights a potential universality in prompt effectiveness.

4.3 Prompts and Models Comparison

As we underlined in the previous sections, the choice of prompt critically influences a model's comprehension and translation of idiomatic expressions. We present an overview of selected translation output, illustrating how influential the prompt choice is on the model's performance. In Table 4, the examples focus on the translation of the Italian idiom "attaccare bottone" (literally translated as "buttoning up") which commonly translates to "striking up a conversation" in English.

Table 4: Translations of "attaccare bottone" using different prompts on the Mistral model, ordered from A to D

Prompt	Translation	COMET
A	You know, he could hit on any girl, anywhere.	76.54
B	You know, he could buttonhole every girl, everywhere and always.	75.76
C	Do you know, he could buttonhole every girl, always and everywhere.	76.77
D	You know, he could get any girl he wanted, anywhere.	**79.55**

While Prompts B and C mistake the intended meaning and generate a literal translation, Prompts A and D align closely to the reference translation and the intended meaning of the Italian idiom. The results we obtain clearly showcase how impactful the prompt choice is on the model's understanding and translation performance.

Building on this, in the following table, we extend the analysis to the OpenAI model, comparing how GPT-3.5 and Mistral handle the same idiomatic input, in their best or worst performance scenario. We display the translation outputs for two Italian idioms: "prendere con le pinze" (literally translated as "to take with tweezers") which idiomatically translates to "to take with a grain of salt" and "avere le mani lunghe" (literally translated as "to have long hands") which translates to "to have sticky fingers".

For the idiom "prendere con le pinze", the Mistral model produced an inaccurate translation, where the subject is missing and the idiomatic expression is translated literally, failing to convey the exact meaning of the input sentence. In contrast, even the least effective prompt with GPT-3.5 provides an accurate and contextually appropriate translation. Mistral is able to accurately translate the idiom, only when prompted by Prompt D. Finally, with the idiom "avere le mani lunghe", both Mistral and GPT-3.5's accurately translate the idiom into two possible correct meanings: Mistral

Table 5: Translations of "Prendere con le pinze" and "Avere le mani lunghe" using different prompts on Mistral and GPT-3.5

Model	Prompt	Translation
Mistral	Worst	Terry, is to be taken with the pliers, ok?
GPT	Worst	Terry, it's to be taken with a grain of salt, okay?
Mistral	Best	You know me, Watson, I'm handsy...
GPT	Best	You know me, Watson, I have sticky fingers...

translates it as being inclined to violence, while GPT-3.5's translation conveys the concept of being inclined to steal with "having sticky fingers".

5 Conclusions

This work presents a preliminary analysis on the use of LLMs for the translation of idiomatic expressions. We find that, given the same dataset and task, identical prompts may have optimal efficacy across various models, as seen for Mistral-7B and GPT-3.5, and that it is possible to optimize the model's performance by choosing an optimal prompt. In our experiments, the five-shot prompt (Prompt D) consistently outperformed other prompts in terms of BLEURT and COMET across both models, over three independent trails, demonstrating the efficacy of leveraging in-context learning ability to improve the model's understanding of idiomatic expressions. As for zero-shot prompting, Prompt C consistently performed the best. We find that GPT-3.5 consistently outperforms Mistral-7B which, on the other hand, can come close to GPT's performance when prompted correctly. Finally, we underline the limitations of traditional metrics based on n-grams, such as BLEU, in evaluating the translation of idiomatic expressions, advocating the use of neural-based evaluation metrics that better capture semantic nuances. Overall, our findings promote a more strategic approach to prompt selection and model use in machine translation, pointing towards a future where LLMs can be used effectively for nuanced and culturally-specific translation tasks. As the field of MT continues to evolve, so too will the strategies for leveraging the full potential of large language models in understanding and translating the rich nuances of human language.

5.1 Limitations

As a preliminary study, there are several aspects that should be improved to make it more comprehensive and reliable. Currently, due to the very specific nature of our task, our evaluation is conducted on a self-compiled dataset of 254 bilingual sentences, presenting only a limited number of idiomatic expressions. For resource and time constraints, the evaluation was only conducted using automated evaluation metrics. Finally, while we have identified that for a given dataset there is an optimal prompt for different models, the underlying factors determining an optimal prompt's performance, given the same task, remain unclear. It is worth noting that our findings are specific to the linguistic context of this evaluation, and the results may differ when applied to other language pairs.

5.2 Future Work

In our future work, we aim to address the current limitations of our study, to make it more reliable and comprehensive by focusing on different areas. First of all, we would like to expand the scope of our research, building a more comprehensive dataset, for a better representation not only of italian idiomatic expressions but also of other features specific of creative text. Regarding prompts, we find it necessary to continue exploring the several prompts that are being researched, such as pivot prompting (Jiao et al., 2023a) and chain-of-dictionary (Lu et al., 2023), and also prompt ensembles, such as those seen in Feng et al. (2024). We deem it necessary to research the best prompting techniques, in order to achieve the very best performance from the models at our disposal, contributing especially to the use of small-scale open-source models, such as the Mistral-7B model we have used in this study. By pursuing these directions, we aim to improve our understanding of how LLMs can be more effectively utilized for the task of translating idiomatic expressions, and more broadly, creative works.

6 Acknowledgements

This work has been funded by the National PhD programme in Artificial Intelligence, partnered by University of Pisa and University of Naples "L'Orientale", through a doctoral grant established by Ex DM 318, of type 4.1, co-financed by the National Recovery and Resilience Plan.

References

Ahuja, Kabir, Harshita Diddee, Rishav Hada, Millicent Ochieng, Krithika Ramesh, Prachi Jain, Akshay Nambi, Tanuja Ganu, Sameer Segal, Maxamed Axmed, Kalika Bali, and Sunayana Sitaram. 2023. MEGA: Multilingual Evaluation of Generative AI. March. arXiv: 2303.12528.

Brown, Tom B., Benjamin Mann, Nick Ryder, Melanie Subbiah, Jared Kaplan, Prafulla Dhariwal, Arvind Neelakantan, Pranav Shyam, Girish Sastry, Amanda Askell, Sandhini Agarwal, Ariel Herbert-Voss, Gretchen Krueger, Tom Henighan, Rewon Child, Aditya Ramesh, Daniel M. Ziegler, Jeffrey Wu, Clemens Winter, Christopher Hesse, Mark Chen, Eric Sigler, Mateusz Litwin, Scott Gray, Benjamin Chess, Jack Clark, Christopher Berner, Sam McCandlish, Alec Radford, Ilya Sutskever, and Dario Amodei. 2020. Language Models are Few-Shot Learners, July. Issue: arXiv:2005.14165 arXiv:2005.14165 [cs].

Eryiğit, GülŞen, Ali Şentaş, and Johanna Monti. 2023. Gamified crowdsourcing for idiom corpora construction. *Natural Language Engineering*, 29(4):909–941, July. Number: 4.

Feng, Zhaopeng, Yan Zhang, Hao Li, Wenqiang Liu, Jun Lang, Yang Feng, Jian Wu, and Zuozhu Liu. 2024. Improving LLM-based Machine Translation with Systematic Self-Correction, March.

Gao, Pengzhi, Zhongjun He, Hua Wu, and Haifeng Wang. 2024. Towards Boosting Many-to-Many Multilingual Machine Translation with Large Language Models, January. Issue: arXiv:2401.05861 arXiv:2401.05861 [cs].

Garcia, Xavier, Yamini Bansal, Colin Cherry, George Foster, Maxim Krikun, Fangxiaoyu Feng, Melvin Johnson, and Orhan Firat. 2023. The unreasonable effectiveness of few-shot learning for machine translation. February. arXiv: 2302.01398.

Guerreiro, Nuno M., Duarte Alves, Jonas Waldendorf, Barry Haddow, Alexandra Birch, Pierre Colombo, and André F. T. Martins. 2023. Hallucinations in Large Multilingual Translation Models. March. arXiv: 2303.16104.

Hendy, Amr, Mohamed Abdelrehim, Amr Sharaf, Vikas Raunak, Mohamed Gabr, Hitokazu Matsushita, Young Jin Kim, Mohamed Afify, and Hany Hassan Awadalla. 2023. How Good Are GPT Models at Machine Translation? A Comprehensive Evaluation. February. arXiv: 2302.09210.

Jiang, Albert Q., Alexandre Sablayrolles, Arthur Mensch, Chris Bamford, Devendra Singh Chaplot, Diego de las Casas, Florian Bressand, Gianna Lengyel, Guillaume Lample, Lucile Saulnier, Lélio Renard Lavaud, Marie-Anne Lachaux, Pierre Stock, Teven Le Scao, Thibaut Lavril, Thomas Wang, Timothée Lacroix, and William El Sayed. 2023. Mistral 7B, October. Issue: arXiv:2310.06825 arXiv:2310.06825 [cs].

Jiao, Wenxiang, Wenxuan Wang, Jen-tse Huang, Xing Wang, Shuming Shi, and Zhaopeng Tu. 2023a. Is ChatGPT A Good Translator? Yes With GPT-4 As The Engine, November.

Jiao, Wenxiang, Wenxuan Wang, Jen-tse Huang, Xing Wang, and Zhaopeng Tu. 2023b. Is ChatGPT A Good Translator? A Preliminary Study. *arXiv*.

Karpinska, Marzena and Mohit Iyyer. 2023. Large language models effectively leverage document-level context for literary translation, but critical errors persist, May. Issue: arXiv:2304.03245 arXiv:2304.03245 [cs].

Lu, Hongyuan, Haoyang Huang, Dongdong Zhang, Haoran Yang, Wai Lam, and Furu Wei. 2023. Chain-of-Dictionary Prompting Elicits Translation in Large Language Models, May. Issue: arXiv:2305.06575 arXiv:2305.06575 [cs].

Mao, Zhuoyuan and Yen Yu. 2024. Tuning LLMs with Contrastive Alignment Instructions for Machine Translation in Unseen, Low-resource Languages, January. Issue: arXiv:2401.05811 arXiv:2401.05811 [cs].

Morza, Giuseppina, Raffaele Manna, and Johanna Monti. 2022. Assessing the Quality of an Italian Crowdsourced Idiom Corpus:the Dodiom Experiment. pages 4205–4211, Marseille, France, June. European Language Resources Association.

Moslem, Yasmin, Rejwanul Haque, John D. Kelleher, and Andy Way. 2023a. Adaptive Machine Translation with Large Language Models. January. arXiv: 2301.13294.

Moslem, Yasmin, Rejwanul Haque, and Andy Way. 2023b. Fine-tuning Large Language Models for Adaptive Machine Translation, December. Issue: arXiv:2312.12740 arXiv:2312.12740 [cs].

Papineni, Kishore, Salim Roukos, Todd Ward, and Wei-Jing Zhu. 2002. Bleu: a Method for Automatic Evaluation of Machine Translation. In Isabelle, Pierre, Eugene Charniak, and Dekang Lin, editors, *Proceedings of the 40th Annual Meeting of the Association for Computational Linguistics*, pages 311–318, Philadelphia, Pennsylvania, USA, July. Association for Computational Linguistics.

Peng, Keqin, Liang Ding, Qihuang Zhong, Li Shen, Xuebo Liu, Min Zhang, Yuanxin Ouyang, and Dacheng Tao. 2023. Towards Making the Most of ChatGPT for Machine Translation. *SSRN Electronic Journal*.

Popović, Maja. 2015. chrF: character n-gram F-score for automatic MT evaluation. In Bojar, Ondřej, Rajan Chatterjee, Christian Federmann, Barry Haddow, Chris Hokamp, Matthias Huck, Varvara Logacheva, and Pavel Pecina, editors, *Proceedings of the Tenth*

Workshop on Statistical Machine Translation, pages 392–395, Lisbon, Portugal, September. Association for Computational Linguistics.

Rei, Ricardo, Craig Stewart, Ana C Farinha, and Alon Lavie. 2020. COMET: A Neural Framework for MT Evaluation. In Webber, Bonnie, Trevor Cohn, Yulan He, and Yang Liu, editors, *Proceedings of the 2020 Conference on Empirical Methods in Natural Language Processing (EMNLP)*, pages 2685–2702, Online, November. Association for Computational Linguistics.

Sellam, Thibault, Dipanjan Das, and Ankur Parikh. 2020. BLEURT: Learning Robust Metrics for Text Generation. In Jurafsky, Dan, Joyce Chai, Natalie Schluter, and Joel Tetreault, editors, *Proceedings of the 58th Annual Meeting of the Association for Computational Linguistics*, pages 7881–7892, Online, July. Association for Computational Linguistics.

Vanroy, Bram, Arda Tezcan, and Lieve Macken. 2023. MATEO: MAchine Translation Evaluation Online. In Nurminen, Mary, Judith Brenner, Maarit Koponen, Sirkku Latomaa, Mikhail Mikhailov, Frederike Schierl, Tharindu Ranasinghe, Eva Vanmassenhove, Sergi Alvarez Vidal, Nora Aranberri, Mara Nunziatini, Carla Parra Escartín, Mikel Forcada, Maja Popovic, Carolina Scarton, and Helena Moniz, editors, *Proceedings of the 24th Annual Conference of the European Association for Machine Translation*, pages 499–500, Tampere, Finland, June. European Association for Machine Translation.

Wang, Longyue, Chenyang Lyu, Tianbo Ji, Zhirui Zhang, Dian Yu, Shuming Shi, and Zhaopeng Tu. 2023. Document-Level Machine Translation with Large Language Models. April. arXiv: 2304.02210.

Wolf, Thomas, Lysandre Debut, Victor Sanh, Julien Chaumond, Clement Delangue, Anthony Moi, Pierric Cistac, Tim Rault, Rémi Louf, Morgan Funtowicz, Joe Davison, Sam Shleifer, Patrick von Platen, Clara Ma, Yacine Jernite, Julien Plu, Canwen Xu, Teven Le Scao, Sylvain Gugger, Mariama Drame, Quentin Lhoest, and Alexander M. Rush. 2020. Huggingface's transformers: State-of-the-art natural language processing.

Wu, Minghao, Thuy-Trang Vu, Lizhen Qu, George Foster, and Gholamreza Haffari. 2024. Adapting Large Language Models for Document-Level Machine Translation, January. Issue: arXiv:2401.06468 arXiv:2401.06468 [cs].

Zhang, Biao, Barry Haddow, and Alexandra Birch. 2023. Prompting Large Language Model for Machine Translation: A Case Study, January. Issue: arXiv:2301.07069 arXiv:2301.07069 [cs].

Zhu, Wenhao, Hongyi Liu, Qingxiu Dong, Jingjing Xu, Shujian Huang, Lingpeng Kong, Jiajun Chen, and Lei Li. 2023. Multilingual Machine Translation with Large Language Models: Empirical Results and Analysis. April. arXiv: 2304.04675.

An Analysis of Surprisal Uniformity in Machine and Human Translations

Josef Jon
Charles University
jon@ufal.mff.cuni.cz

Ondřej Bojar
Charles University
bojar@ufal.mff.cuni.cz

Abstract

This study examines neural machine translation (NMT) and its performance on texts that diverege from typical standards, focusing on how information is organized within sentences.

We analyze surprisal distributions in source texts, human translations, and machine translations across several datasets to determine if NMT systems naturally promote a uniform density of surprisal in their translations, even when the original texts do not adhere to this principle. The findings reveal that NMT tends to align more closely with source texts in terms of surprisal uniformity compared to human translations. We analyzed absolute values of the surprisal uniformity measures as well, expecting that human translations will be less uniform. In contradiction to our initial hypothesis, we did not find comprehensive evidence for this claim, with some results suggesting this might be the case for very diverse texts, like poetry.

1 Introduction

Natural language processing tools based on machine learning, such as machine translation, autocorrect, predictive typing, search, and text generation, have become integral to our daily lives. With the advancement of Large Language Models (LLMs), it's anticipated that interacting with these technologies will become a critical aspect of our work and societal engagement. However, numerous questions about these technologies persist. In this work, we take a look specifically at neural machine translation (NMT) and at one such question: How well do these tools work on an input that is different from a typical text, not in terminology or domain, but in a way the information content is organized within an utterance? Are there any biases within the algorithms themselves that can be beneficial for ordinary types of texts, but harmful for specific cases that deviate from the usual rules found in mundane text content?

We propose that Neural Machine Translation (NMT) will be more effective with texts adhering to the Uniform Information Density (UID; (Levy and Jaeger, 2006)) hypothesis, meaning that the level of surprisal is consistently spread out throughout the sequence. One of the culprits could be the beam search decoding, which has been shown to adhere to the UID principle (Meister et al., 2020), i.e. even if the input has a diverse distribution of surprisal, the distribution in the translation will be more uniform. The UID-enforcing property of beam search has been shown as the key to its ability to produce high-quality, human-like texts (compared to exact search under the same model), even being dubbed the *beam search blessing* by (Meister et al., 2020).

We hypothesize that while in general, this property is positive, there are use-cases where too much emphasis on the uniformity of suprisals hurts the final translation quality. In this work, we look for such examples by comparing distributions of suprisals over source texts, machine translation and human translation across multiple test sets.

Proceedings of the 1st Workshop on Creative-text Translation and Technology, pages 40–56
June 27, 2024 ©2024 European Association for Machine Translation

2 Related work

In this section, we will list the work exploring the presence of the UID principle in human-produced language as well as its presence and links to MT algorithms.

There is an extensive body of psycholinguistic work concerning the relationship between text predictability or surprisal and reading comprehension. The results on whether the effects of surprisal on reading comprehension is linear or super-linear (which would be consistent with the UID hypothesis) are mixed: For example, (Meister et al., 2021; Hoover et al., 2023) found support for super-linear relationship.

One of the most recent and largest studies (Shain et al., 2024) uses a wide array of open-source datasets, new Large Language Models for the surprisal estimation (GPT-3) and novel evaluation methods (deep learning based non-linear regression for analyzing continuous-time systems (Shain and Schuler, 2023). Their findings support a linear relationship between word surprisal and sentence reading times, suggesting that any pressure for UID seen in natural language is not motivated by an easier comprehension.

(Meister et al., 2020) ask why, empirically, beam search produces higher quality outputs than exacted search under the same model. To find the inductive bias embedded in beam search that allows this, they reverse engineer the objective that beam search is a solution for. They found that beam search can be reformulated as an exact search with a uniformity regularizer which enforces UID and that this property is the key to its effectivity. (Wei et al., 2021) employ a similar regularizer in the training of the model, which led to improved translation quality.

3 Methods

This section introduces the measures we use to operationalize the surprisal distribution uniformity concept, closely following the definition by (Meister et al., 2021).

3.1 Uniform information density

Surprisal theory, as outlined by (Hale, 2001), establishes a direct relationship between cognitive effort and the surprisal value of words; in other words, the effort required to comprehend a word is directly proportional to its level of predictability within a given context. To elaborate, for any given utterance, denoted as $\mathbf{u}$ and consisting of elements (e.g. words) u_n, the surprisal of each element can be calculated as $s(u_n) = -\log p(u_n|\mathbf{u}_{<n})$, i.e. negative log-probability of the word given the previous context. Therefore, the total cognitive effort needed can be represented as

$$\text{Effort}(u_n) \propto s(u_n)$$

Suppose we apply the same approach to a longer sequence of words, such as a sentence. In that case, we arrive to a counter-intuitive conclusion: If the surprisal of the sentence is a sum of surprisals of particular words and this sentence-level surprisal is predictive of processing effort (e.g. reading time), then any way of distributing the information across the utterance is the same in terms of the effort needed for comprehension.

To address this counter-intuitive consequence, the Uniform Information Density theory (UID) suggests a super-linear relationship between the surprisal levels of units and the total effort involved, incorporating the length of the utterance, denoted as N, into its framework (Aylett and Turk, 2004; Fenk and Fenk-Oczlon, 1980; Levy and Jaeger, 2006; Bell et al., 2003; Genzel and Charniak, 2002):

$$\text{Effort}(\mathbf{u}) \propto \sum_{n=1}^{N} s\left(u_n\right)^k + c \cdot N, k > 1$$

This definition suggests that utterances with a more uniform distribution of surprisal are simpler for human comprehension, indicating a preference for evenly spreading surprisal to effectively communicate a message.

We will demonstrate the intuitive concept of surprisal uniformity on the following two sentences:

- **A) More uniform:** *"When she got home after a long day at work, she decided to relax by reading her favorite novel and having a cup of tea."*
- **B) Less uniform:** *"London's annual festival was filled with activities, food stands, windsurfing, and drinks, but the sudden unveiling of a Yetti statue caught everyone's attention."*

Most people would consider the second sentence as more surprising, some of the words feel unexpected. We show the surprisal profiles of both sentences in Figure 1. Indeed, we can see that the

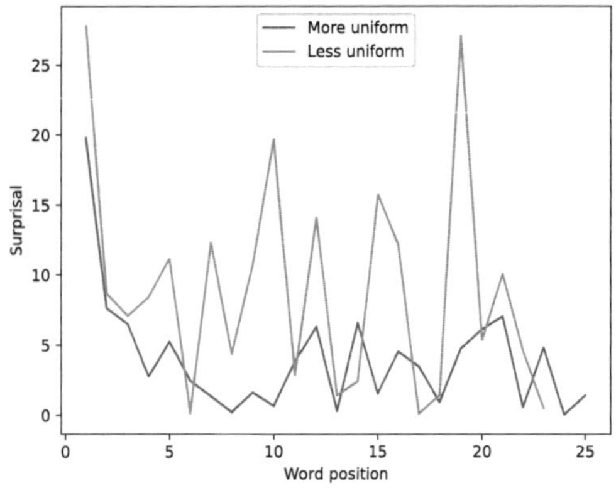

Figure 1: Surprisal behavior for the two examples sentences, measured by GPT-2 model.

surprisal behavior of the second sentence (orange) looks less uniform.

To express the uniformity as a measurable quantity, we experiment with multiple formulas, like Local Variance (LV), Coefficient of Variation (CV), Global Variance (GV), Gini coefficient, and Super-linear Relationship (SL), and super-linear syntactic log-odds ratio (SLOR, (Kann et al., 2018; Pauls and Klein, 2012)):

- $\mathrm{LV}(\mathbf{u}) = \frac{1}{N-1} \sum_{n=2}^{N} \left(s\left(u_n\right) - s\left(u_{n-1}\right)\right)^2$
- $\mathrm{CV}(\mathbf{u}) = \frac{\sigma(\mathbf{u})}{\mu(\mathbf{u})}$
- $\mathrm{GV}(\mathbf{u}) = \frac{1}{N} \sum_{n=1}^{N} \left(s\left(u_n\right) - \mu(corpus)\right)^2$
- $\mathrm{SL}(\mathbf{u}) = \frac{1}{N} \sum_{n=1}^{N} s\left(u_n\right)^k \quad (k > 1)$
- $\mathrm{SLOR}(\mathbf{u}) = \frac{1}{N} \sum_{n=1}^{N} s\left(u_n\right)^k - s_u\left(u_n\right)^k \quad (k > 1)$

Function s denotes surprisal in of a word in context, s_n is a unigram, context-free surprisal.

3.2 Surprisal distribution and translation

We hypothesize that the uniform distribution of surprisal is implicitly enforced by algorithms used for training and decoding in NMT, most prominently by the beam search (see (Meister et al., 2020) for the rationalization). In practical terms, we suggest that source texts characterized by highly uneven surprisal distributions would maintain such distribution upon translation by a human, but translation by MT engine would result in a more uniform distribution. We conducted measurements across multiple datasets, employing the uniformity measures described in the previous section.

4 Results

This section describes the settings and presents the results of measuring difference in surprisal uniformity in human and machine translations.

4.1 Models and Datasets

The first part of our investigation into the uniformity of surprisal across source texts, human translations, and machine translations focuses on the English-French language pair. We utilize a diverse set of corpora: the Books corpus (Zhu et al., 2015) (*books*), Global Voices (Nguyen and Daumé III, 2019) (*global*), Newstest2014 (Bojar et al., 2014) (*wmt*), and a French translation of a poem by Oscar Wilde translated by Jean Guiloineau (*wilde*). For the next set of experiments, involving multiple reference translations in English-Czech direction, we draw upon the dataset provided by (Zouhar and Bojar, 2024; Zouhar et al., 2023), which we refer to as *ORT*.

For comparing surprisals in English to French translations, we turn to `BLOOM-1B7` (BigScience Workshop, 2022) for our estimates. For the analysis involving Czech translations with multiple references, surprisal estimates are obtained from `MU-NLPC/CzeGPT-2` (Hájek and Horák, 2024) and `BUT-FIT/Czech-GPT-2-XL-133k` (Fajčík et al., 2024).

Machine translation (MT) systems are also used in our experiments: In the case of English to French translations, Google Translate (`mt1`) and `facebook/nllb-200-distilled-600M` (Team et al., 2022) as (`mt2`) serve as our MT systems. For English to Czech tasks, translations are provided by Google Translate (`mt1`) and one of the top-performing systems from WMT22 (Jon et al., 2022) as `mt2`. We are aware that using an external MT engine harms the replicability of the experiments. On the other hand, we wanted to analyze if our hypothesis applied to real-world, non-NLP community scenarios, where similar engines are often used.

4.2 Results

We studied how some of the uniformity measures change during the translation process, both for human (HT) and machine translation (MT). Surprisal estimates, obtained using models detailed in Section 4.1, are measured on a word level without tokenization, i.e. they consider punctuation as part of adjacent words. Additional results, with including tokenization and excluding punctuation surprisals, are available in Appendix A.1. The initial word's surprisal is excluded due to unreliable first token estimates from GPT-style models, though similar results were observed when included.

dataset	measure	HT	MT1	MT2
books	LV^2	0.39	0.58	0.42
	CV	0.42	0.51	0.50
	GV^2	0.46	0.69	0.54
wmt	LV^2	0.43	0.54	0.58
	CV	0.49	0.55	0.57
	GV^2	0.46	0.57	0.64
global	LV^2	0.69	0.73	0.78
	CV	0.65	0.70	0.63
	GV^2	0.72	0.74	0.80
global_doc	LV^2	0.72	0.79	0.83
	CV	0.68	0.81	0.82
	GV^2	0.76	0.83	0.86
wilde	LV^2	0.16	0.40	0.53
	CV	0.07	0.39	0.54
	GV^2	0.16	0.40	0.53

Table 1: Pearsons' r for sentence-level surprisal uniformity of measurements between source and either HT, MT1 or MT2.

For conciseness, we present the results on three measures: local variance squared (LV^2), sentence-level coefficient of variation (CV), and global variance squared (GV^2), with global variance calculated as the mean across all surprisals in the text or translation. Detailed findings for other measures are presented in Appendix A.1.

Table 1 presents Pearson's r, comparing sentence-level surprisal uniformity between the source and HT or MT, showcasing that MT aligns more closely with source text surprisal distribution than HT across all datasets and measures. In Appendix A.1, we also show the scatter plots of values of the measures for source sentence and either HT, MT1 or MT2 across datasets.

This result suggests that the source's distribution of surprisal is followed more closely by an MT system than a human translator, at least on a sentence level. We hypothesized that the human translators do not translate the sentences one by one in isolation and might distribute the surprisal variance in larger text units. This is the reason why we also measured the uniformity on a document level in *global_doc*, treating each document as a single sequence of tokens for the purposes of surprisal estimation. The results do not support our hypothesis – surprisal distribution uniformity of MT is still better correlated with the source than in HT.

Absolute values of the uniformity measures (Table 2a) indicate MT is generally (with some exceptions, depending on the measure and the dataset) as uniform or less uniform than HT. Historgrams of the values support the same conclusion and are shown in the Appendix. This contradicts our initial hypothesis that MT will be more uniform in surprisal. We explored whether translation errors could cause an increase in surprisal diversity in MT – if the MT system translates the input with some obvious mistakes, then these mistakes might be very surprising given the rest of the sentence. We used reference-free COMET (`wmt22-cometkiwi-da`, (Rei et al., 2022)) scores to assess translation quality. We note that this approach is not without issues – COMET scores have been shown as unreliable on segment-level (Moghe et al., 2022).

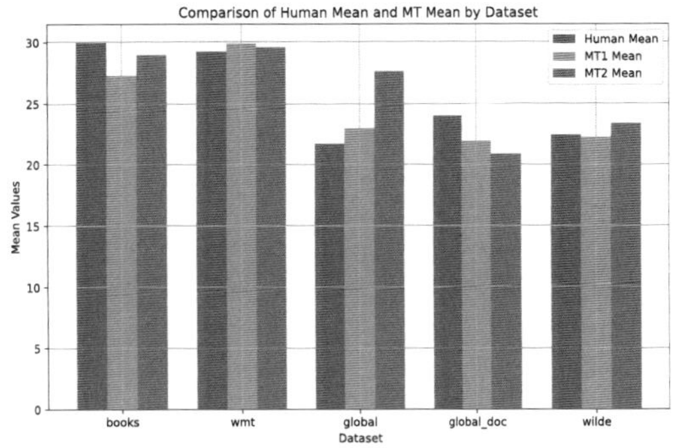

Figure 2: Comparison on HT, MT1, and MT2 LV^2 scores per dataset (whole datasets, without MT quality filtering).

Figure 3 shows the behavior of the value of LV^2 measure for examples where the MT COMET score is above the threshold (the threshold is on the x-axis). We see that the uniformity behavior is consistent between the HT (green) and the MT (blue and orange), except for the *wilde* dataset, where the unevenness of HT is higher when we only consider the better-scoring sentences. This result might suggest that for very creative texts (such as poetry), MT is more uniform than a human if we disregard wrongly translated utterances.

The plots show another interesting property – the COMET scores are the highest for the most uniform sentences. Since we select the examples based on the COMET scores for the MT in these plots, it can be interpreted as a property of the MT system: it translates the most uniform sentences the best. However, this behavior in the plots is very similar even when the COMET scores are computed for the HT (see Appendix A.1), suggesting a

dataset	m	$\mu(s)$	$\rho(s)$	$\mu(ht)$	$\rho(ht)$	$\mu(mt1)$	$\rho(mt1)$	$\mu(mt2)$	$\rho(mt2)$
books	LV^2	31.9	29.6	30.2	30.6	28.0	29.0	29.3	23.4
	CV	0.72	0.17	0.71	0.18	0.73	0.18	0.73	0.16
	GV^2	20.2	25.1	21.3	31.0	21.1	30.0	20.8	20.4
wmt	LV^2	28.1	16.6	22.5	13.2	22.5	13.3	23.5	13.8
	CV	0.76	0.16	0.80	0.16	0.81	0.17	0.80	0.16
	GV^2	18.1	13.0	15.4	9.2	15.8	9.9	15.8	9.5
global	LV^2	33.0	32.5	29.3	32.1	30.2	34.9	29.8	30.2
	CV	0.73	0.21	0.75	0.21	0.79	0.22	0.78	0.21
	GV^2	22.5	24.6	21.7	27.2	21.8	27.8	20.9	22.8
global_doc	LV^2	26.6	5.9	22.1	5.4	23.4	5.5	24.3	17.1
	CV	0.94	0.07	0.98	0.08	1.00	0.09	1.17	0.49
	GV^2	15.2	3.3	13.1	3.2	13.9	3.2	16.5	9.7
wilde	LV^2	29.7	12.1	26.0	10.0	26.7	11.5	25.3	10.5
	CV	0.67	0.08	0.63	0.09	0.69	0.10	0.72	0.11
	GV^2	16.0	5.7	15.1	5.2	14.6	5.5	13.4	5.4

(a) Uniformity measures for source, MT and HT across datasets for whole datasets, including examples of poor MT quality.

dataset	m	$\mu(s)$	$\rho(s)$	$\mu(ht)$	$\rho(ht)$	$\mu(mt1)$	$\rho(mt1)$	$\mu(mt2)$	$\rho(mt2)$
books	LV^2	30.4	27.7	30.1	32.6	27.1	26.0	28.9	24.0
	CV	0.72	0.17	0.71	0.18	0.73	0.18	0.73	0.16
	GV^2	19.6	24.4	21.8	34.3	21.1	29.6	21.0	21.3
wmt	LV^2	25.6	14.4	20.7	12.3	20.3	11.1	21.1	12.1
	CV	0.78	0.16	0.82	0.17	0.84	0.16	0.82	0.16
	GV^2	16.8	10.5	14.7	8.5	14.8	8.8	14.8	8.6
global	LV^2	32.9	32.6	29.2	32.2	29.9	34.8	29.6	30.2
	CV	0.73	0.20	0.76	0.21	0.79	0.21	0.78	0.20
	GV^2	22.2	24.3	21.5	27.1	21.5	27.4	20.8	22.4
global_doc	LV^2	26.4	7.1	21.8	6.3	23.2	6.7	26.5	18.6
	CV	0.96	0.08	1.00	0.09	1.03	0.11	1.10	0.27
	GV^2	15.3	3.8	13.3	3.8	14.0	3.9	17.4	12.3
wilde	LV^2	25.4	10.7	24.5	8.9	21.7	9.1	21.0	7.0
	CV	0.69	0.08	0.64	0.09	0.69	0.10	0.72	0.10
	GV^2	14.0	3.9	14.7	4.7	12.7	4.0	11.7	2.8

(b) Uniformity measures for source, MT and HT across datasets, with manually set COMET thresholds for each dataset to only select examples with high quality MT.

different underlying cause, for example, COMET bias to score more uniform sentences higher. Such biases are a base for further investigation since they do not allow us to directly automatically compare translation quality between diverse and non-diverse texts (i.e. if one system's translations are more uniform, they could be unfairly scored better than less uniform translations). This property diminishes the validity of our approach to filtering and in future work, we will focus on better ways of selecting high-quality translations for evaluation. For GV^2 score, the behavior is similar, however, we see a different trend for CV (Appendix A.1).

Based on our inspection of the translations, we have chosen COMET thresholds for which the translations seem acceptable, without serious translation errors. These thresholds are dataset specific, since COMET scores are domain dependent.[1]. The results are presented in Table 2b. Again, the only notable difference to the whole dataset is on the *wilde* test set, where HT is less uniform (in LV^2) considering only examples with high-quality MT.

4.3 Multiple references

In this analysis, we explore how translation processes, both human (ref) and machine (mt), affect the uniformity of surprisal distributions, utilizing the ORT dataset to compare multiple high-quality human translations against machine translations. Surprisal estimates were generated using the `MU-NLPC/CzeGPT-2` model, with parallel ex-

[1]The thresholds are: `wmt: 0.88, books: 0.81, global: 0.7, wilde: 0.72, global_doc: 0.65`

metric	src	ref1	ref2	ref3	ref4	mt	mt2
$\mu(s^{0.25})$	1.72	1.49	1.49	**1.53**	1.48	1.51	1.52
$\rho(s^{0.25})$	0.08	0.10	0.09	0.10	0.10	0.10	0.10
$\mu(s)$	10.21	7.07	6.91	**7.73**	6.94	7.13	7.59
$\rho(s)$	1.62	1.87	1.57	**1.97**	1.85	1.70	1.96
$\mu(s^3)$	2797	2902	1939	3289	2862	2130	**3290**
$\rho(s^3)$	1497	3455	2546	3615	3487	2763	**3663**
$\mu(gini)$	0.33	**0.45**	0.42	0.44	**0.45**	0.42	0.44
$\rho(gini)$	0.05	0.07	0.06	0.07	0.07	0.07	0.07
$\mu(CV)$	0.62	0.94	0.85	0.90	**0.95**	0.84	0.92
$\rho(CV)$	0.11	0.23	0.19	0.22	**0.24**	0.19	0.23
$\mu(LV^2)$	70.6	83.5	62.7	92.8	83.0	65.1	**93.2**
$\rho(LV^2)$	30.4	83.6	65.3	84.6	**85.3**	65.5	82.4
$\mu(GV^2)$	42.0	53.7	40.3	**58.2**	53.2	41.1	**58.2**
$\rho(GV^2)$	18.7	47.6	36.1	47.9	**48.2**	35.4	47.2

Table 3: Mean values and standard deviations of sentenece-level uniformity measures for source, two machine translations and the three human reference sets. The texts are not tokenized for the surprisal estimation, thus the estimates for punctuation are often summed up with the adjacent words in the calculations of the uniformity metrics. Across most of the metrics, *ref2* and *mt* are the most uniform translations.

metric	src	ref1	ref2	ref3	ref4	mt	mt2
$\mu(s^{0.25})$	1.72	1.45	1.47	1.51	1.45	1.48	1.48
$\rho(s^{0.25})$	0.08	0.10	0.09	0.11	0.09	0.09	0.09
$\mu(s)$	10.34	6.50	6.57	7.52	6.48	6.55	6.85
$\rho(s)$	1.59	1.77	1.62	2.19	1.75	1.34	1.41
$\mu(s^3)$	2738	2422	1802	3445	2436	1565	2340
$\rho(s^3)$	1388	3958	3336	4176	4102	2479	2953
$\mu(gini)$	0.32	0.45	0.43	0.45	0.45	0.41	0.44
$\rho(gini)$	0.06	0.08	0.07	0.08	0.07	0.07	0.08
$\mu(CV)$	0.60	0.94	0.86	0.93	0.93	0.83	0.90
$\rho(CV)$	0.13	0.25	0.20	0.23	0.24	0.21	0.24
$\mu(LV^2)$	68.0	71.8	60.6	96.6	73.2	52.9	73.0
$\rho(LV^2)$	32.1	99.7	88.8	98.6	105.8	58.7	70.9
$\mu(GV^2)$	40.4	47.7	38.7	61.8	47.6	34.2	46.7
$\rho(GV^2)$	18.3	51.5	44.3	54.0	53.8	31.8	39.2

Table 4: Mean values and standard deviations of sentenece-level uniformity measures for source, two machine translations and the three human reference sets, using only examples where COMET score is above 0.88 for both `mt` and `mt2`.

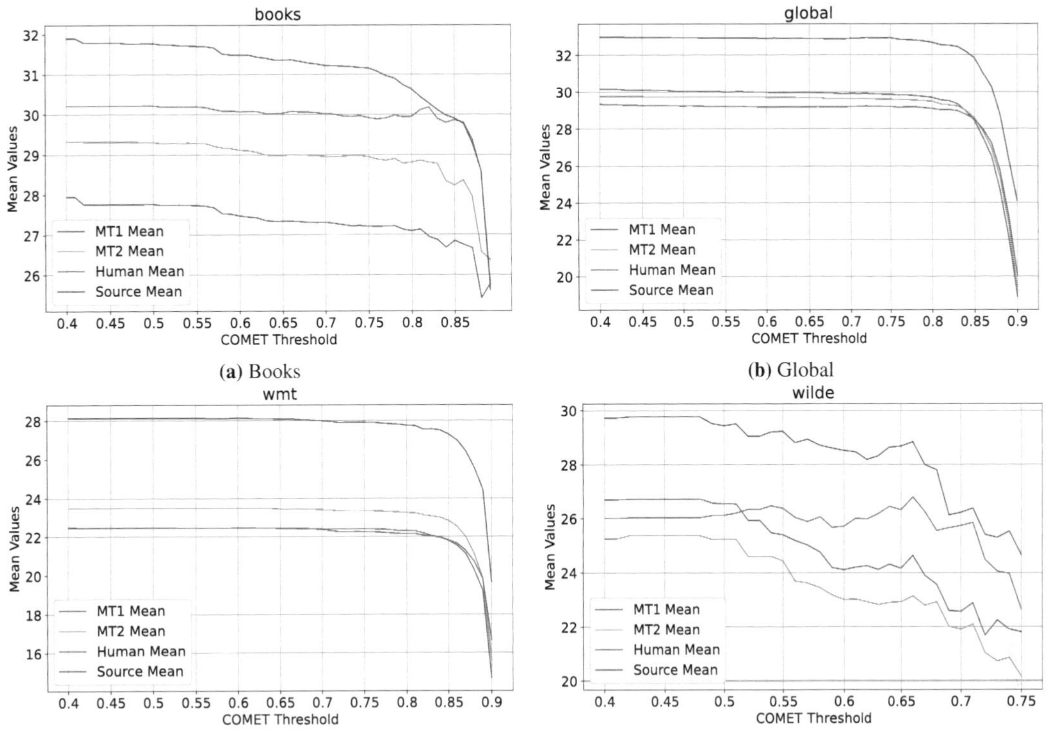

(a) Books (b) Global (c) WMT (d) Wilde

Figure 3: Relationship between COMET scores of the MT and the LV^2 measure. As a proxy of translation quality, we use COMET score threshold to filter out low-quality translations.

periments conducted using an alternative language model (`BUT-FIT/Czech-GPT-2-XL-133k`) for comparison, detailed in Appendix A.1.3.

Figure 4 presents Pearson's r for three uniformity measures (LV^2, CV, GV^2), revealing the degree of correlation between the source and translations.

Table 3 summarizes the mean values and standard deviations of sentence-level uniformity measures, showing variations across source, human, and machine translations. We see that `mt` usually scores as the most uniform, while `mt2` is among the least uniform translations, showing large variance among different MT systems.

Again, we seek to filter out translation errors in MT which could increase the diversity of surprisals by producing expressions unrelated to the rest of the sentences. This approach allows for a focused analysis on translations that accurately convey the source text's meaning without significant errors, which could otherwise distort the surprisal distribution. Upon inspection of the translations, we set the COMET threshold to 0.88 for both mt and mt2 simultaneously. Figure 5 shows the LV^2 measure for both the unfiltered and filtered datasets. Similar bar charts for CV and GV^2 scores can be found in Appendix A.1.3. We see that `mt1` usually scores as the most uniform, while `mt2` is among the least uniform translations, showing large variance among different MT systems. We see that while `mt2` is the most diverse translation for the whole dataset, after filtering out the lower quality translations, `ref3` becomes the most diverse in terms of LV^2 score. This result again suggests that at least a part of the surprisal diversity of MT is caused by translation errors.

5 Future work

The results of our study are inconclusive and we plan to obtain more diverse test sets, where the MT adherence to generating uniform texts could be harmful. Suppose we find such texts, where traditional, encoder-decoder MT models using beam search decoding struggle. In that case, we will evaluate also large language models, where the decoding algorithm is usually based on sampling.

We speculate that the constraints on surprisal distribution imposed by beam search might be

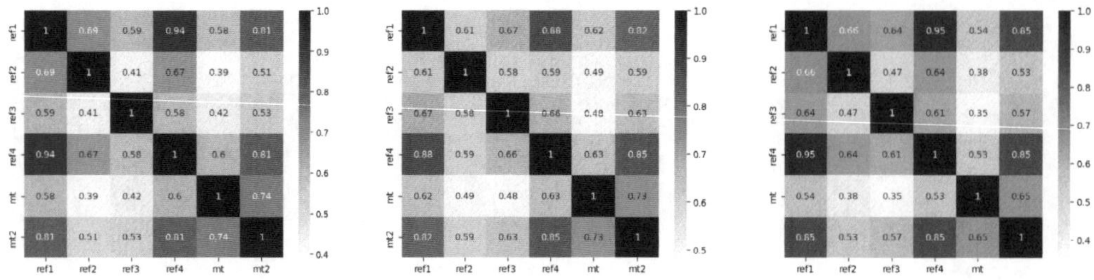

(a) Local variance squared (b) Sentence CV (c) Global variance squared

Figure 4: Correlation coefficients (Pearson's r) of three sentence-level measures of uniformity across the source texts, four human references and the machine translation.

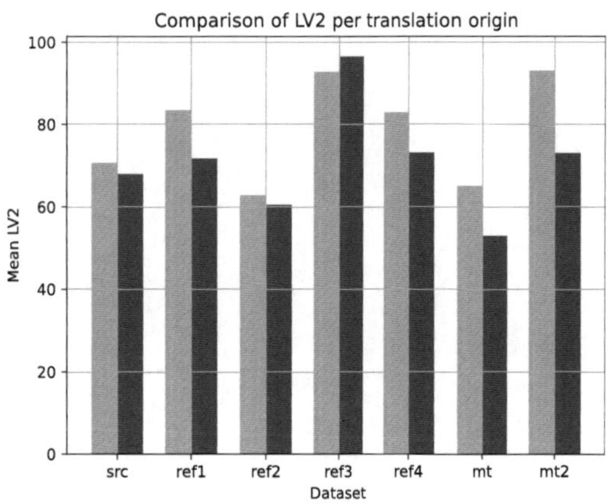

Figure 5: Difference of LV^2 scores between all (orange) and high-quality (green) MT translations.

compensating for the models' inherent lack of global planning. In an ideal scenario, a model might introduce a word with high surprisal intentionally, planning to balance this with lower surprisal words in subsequent segments. However, the current model designs, focusing on next-token prediction, might not accurately forecast these future steps, i.e. the model could produce high surprisal word with a "plan" to get the surprisal "back" in the future timesteps, but, due to next-token-only objective, the future steps are miscalculated. The beam search will not produce such word, due to the adherence to the local uniformity, so the modelling flaw stays hidden.

If this hypothesis turns out to be true, our focus will shift to improve the global planning capabilities of the models, e.g. by employing an alternative training objective.

6 Conclusions

Overall, we do not have reliable proof that MT produces texts that are more uniform in surprisal distribution than humans yet. Either our hypothesis is false, or our measurement methodology is flawed. One possible reason could be that the LMs we used to estimate the surprisals are trained on human text, not on MT outputs so it overestimates surprisal of some phenomena in MT. We plan further experiments to improve our methodology and extend the analysis to more datasets.

While our study was not able to reliably prove our initial hypothesis that MT systems make the distribution of surprisal more uniform in their translations than a human translator, we have gained some insights from the experiments we carried out. Firstly, NMT systems demonstrate a tendency to produce translations that exhibit surprisal uniformity closely aligned with source texts, more so than a human translator. Secondly, the absolute values of uniformity measures are similar between HT and MT as well, however, it depends on the MT system used. Some of the systems produce more uniform translations than humans.

Notably, in more varied datasets, such as those containing literary works or poetry, human translations showed greater diversity compared to MT outputs, according to some of the measures.

Some of the findings indicate that part of the variance in surprisal distribution observed in MT may stem from translation inaccuracies. By scoring the translations using quality estimation metrics and filtering out low-scoring examples, in MT surprisal uniformity on one of the datasets increases, while HT uniformity stays the same.

7 Acknowledgements

This work was supported by the Grant Agency of Charles University in Prague (GAUK 244523) and by the Ministry of Education, Youth and Sports of the Czech Republic through the e-INFRA CZ (ID:90254).

References

Aylett, Matthew and Alice Turk. 2004. The smooth signal redundancy hypothesis: A functional explanation for relationships between redundancy, prosodic prominence, and duration in spontaneous speech. *Language and Speech*, 47(1):31–56. PMID: 15298329.

Bell, Alan, Daniel Jurafsky, Eric Fosler-Lussier, Cynthia Girand, Michelle Gregory, and Daniel Gildea. 2003. Effects of disfluencies, predictability, and utterance position on word form variation in English conversation. *The Journal of the Acoustical Society of America*, 113(2):1001–1024, 01.

BigScience Workshop. 2022. BLOOM (revision 4ab0472).

Bojar, Ondřej, Christian Buck, Christian Federmann, Barry Haddow, Philipp Koehn, Johannes Leveling, Christof Monz, Pavel Pecina, Matt Post, Herve Saint-Amand, Radu Soricut, Lucia Specia, and Aleš Tamchyna. 2014. Findings of the 2014 workshop on statistical machine translation. In Bojar, Ondřej, Christian Buck, Christian Federmann, Barry Haddow, Philipp Koehn, Christof Monz, Matt Post, and Lucia Specia, editors, *Proceedings of the Ninth Workshop on Statistical Machine Translation*, pages 12–58, Baltimore, Maryland, USA, June. Association for Computational Linguistics.

Fajčík, Martin, Martin Dočekal, Jan Doležal, Karel Beneš, and Michal Hradiš. 2024. Benczechmark: Machine language understanding benchmark for czech language. *arXiv preprint arXiv:insert-arxiv-number-here*, March.

Fenk, August and Gertraud Fenk-Oczlon. 1980. Konstanz im kurzzeitgedächtnis - konstanz im sprachlichen informationsfluß? *Zeitschrift für experimentelle und angewandte Psychologie*, 27:400–414, 01.

Genzel, Dmitriy and Eugene Charniak. 2002. Entropy rate constancy in text. In Isabelle, Pierre, Eugene Charniak, and Dekang Lin, editors, *Proceedings of the 40th Annual Meeting of the Association for Computational Linguistics*, pages 199–206, Philadelphia, Pennsylvania, USA, July. Association for Computational Linguistics.

Hale, John. 2001. A probabilistic Earley parser as a psycholinguistic model. In *Second Meeting of the North American Chapter of the Association for Computational Linguistics*.

Hoover, Jacob Louis, Morgan Sonderegger, Steven T. Piantadosi, and Timothy J. O'Donnell. 2023. The Plausibility of Sampling as an Algorithmic Theory of Sentence Processing. *Open Mind*, 7:350–391, 07.

Hájek, Adam and Aleš Horák. 2024. Czegpt-2 – training new model for czech generative text processing evaluated with the summarization task. *IEEE Access*, 12:34570–34581.

Jon, Josef, Martin Popel, and Ondřej Bojar. 2022. CUNI-bergamot submission at WMT22 general translation task. In Koehn, Philipp, Loïc Barrault, Ondřej Bojar, Fethi Bougares, Rajen Chatterjee, Marta R. Costa-jussà, Christian Federmann, Mark Fishel, Alexander Fraser, Markus Freitag, Yvette Graham, Roman Grundkiewicz, Paco Guzman, Barry Haddow, Matthias Huck, Antonio Jimeno Yepes, Tom Kocmi, André Martins, Makoto Morishita, Christof Monz, Masaaki Nagata, Toshiaki Nakazawa, Matteo Negri, Aurélie Névéol, Mariana Neves, Martin Popel, Marco Turchi, and Marcos Zampieri, editors, *Proceedings of the Seventh Conference on Machine Translation (WMT)*, pages 280–289, Abu Dhabi, United Arab Emirates (Hybrid), December. Association for Computational Linguistics.

Kann, Katharina, Sascha Rothe, and Katja Filippova. 2018. Sentence-level fluency evaluation: References help, but can be spared! In Korhonen, Anna and Ivan Titov, editors, *Proceedings of the 22nd Conference on Computational Natural Language Learning*, pages 313–323, Brussels, Belgium, October. Association for Computational Linguistics.

Levy, Roger and T. Florian Jaeger. 2006. Speakers optimize information density through syntactic reduction. volume 19, pages 849–856, 01.

Meister, Clara, Ryan Cotterell, and Tim Vieira. 2020. If beam search is the answer, what was the question? In Webber, Bonnie, Trevor Cohn, Yulan He, and Yang Liu, editors, *Proceedings of the 2020 Conference on Empirical Methods in Natural Language Processing (EMNLP)*, pages 2173–2185, Online, November. Association for Computational Linguistics.

Meister, Clara, Tiago Pimentel, Patrick Haller, Lena Jäger, Ryan Cotterell, and Roger Levy. 2021. Revisiting the Uniform Information Density hypothesis. In Moens, Marie-Francine, Xuanjing Huang, Lucia Specia, and Scott Wen-tau Yih, editors, *Proceedings of the 2021 Conference on Empirical Methods in Natural Language Processing*, pages 963–980, Online and Punta Cana, Dominican Republic, November. Association for Computational Linguistics.

Moghe, Nikita, Tom Sherborne, Mark Steedman, and Alexandra Birch. 2022. Extrinsic evaluation of machine translation metrics.

Nguyen, Khanh and Hal Daumé III. 2019. Global Voices: Crossing borders in automatic news summarization. In Wang, Lu, Jackie Chi Kit Cheung, Giuseppe Carenini, and Fei Liu, editors, *Proceedings of the 2nd Workshop on New Frontiers in Summarization*, pages 90–97, Hong Kong, China, November. Association for Computational Linguistics.

Pauls, Adam and Dan Klein. 2012. Large-scale syntactic language modeling with treelets. In Li, Haizhou, Chin-Yew Lin, Miles Osborne, Gary Geunbae Lee, and Jong C. Park, editors, *Proceedings of the 50th*

Annual Meeting of the Association for Computational Linguistics (Volume 1: Long Papers), pages 959–968, Jeju Island, Korea, July. Association for Computational Linguistics.

Rei, Ricardo, Marcos Treviso, Nuno M. Guerreiro, Chrysoula Zerva, Ana C Farinha, Christine Maroti, José G. C. de Souza, Taisiya Glushkova, Duarte Alves, Luisa Coheur, Alon Lavie, and André F. T. Martins. 2022. CometKiwi: IST-unbabel 2022 submission for the quality estimation shared task. In Koehn, Philipp, Loïc Barrault, Ondřej Bojar, Fethi Bougares, Rajen Chatterjee, Marta R. Costa-jussà, Christian Federmann, Mark Fishel, Alexander Fraser, Markus Freitag, Yvette Graham, Roman Grundkiewicz, Paco Guzman, Barry Haddow, Matthias Huck, Antonio Jimeno Yepes, Tom Kocmi, André Martins, Makoto Morishita, Christof Monz, Masaaki Nagata, Toshiaki Nakazawa, Matteo Negri, Aurélie Névéol, Mariana Neves, Martin Popel, Marco Turchi, and Marcos Zampieri, editors, *Proceedings of the Seventh Conference on Machine Translation (WMT)*, pages 634–645, Abu Dhabi, United Arab Emirates (Hybrid), December. Association for Computational Linguistics.

Shain, Cory and William Schuler. 2023. A deep learning approach to analyzing continuous-time systems.

Shain, Cory, Clara Meister, Tiago Pimentel, Ryan Cotterell, and Roger Levy. 2024. Large-scale evidence for logarithmic effects of word predictability on reading time. *Proceedings of the National Academy of Sciences*, 121(10):e2307876121.

Team, NLLB, Marta R. Costa-jussà, James Cross, Onur Çelebi, Maha Elbayad, Kenneth Heafield, Kevin Heffernan, Elahe Kalbassi, Janice Lam, Daniel Licht, Jean Maillard, Anna Sun, Skyler Wang, Guillaume Wenzek, Al Youngblood, Bapi Akula, Loic Barrault, Gabriel Mejia Gonzalez, Prangthip Hansanti, John Hoffman, Semarley Jarrett, Kaushik Ram Sadagopan, Dirk Rowe, Shannon Spruit, Chau Tran, Pierre Andrews, Necip Fazil Ayan, Shruti Bhosale, Sergey Edunov, Angela Fan, Cynthia Gao, Vedanuj Goswami, Francisco Guzmán, Philipp Koehn, Alexandre Mourachko, Christophe Ropers, Safiyyah Saleem, Holger Schwenk, and Jeff Wang. 2022. No language left behind: Scaling human-centered machine translation.

Wei, Jason, Clara Meister, and Ryan Cotterell. 2021. A cognitive regularizer for language modeling. In Zong, Chengqing, Fei Xia, Wenjie Li, and Roberto Navigli, editors, *Proceedings of the 59th Annual Meeting of the Association for Computational Linguistics and the 11th International Joint Conference on Natural Language Processing (Volume 1: Long Papers)*, pages 5191–5202, Online, August. Association for Computational Linguistics.

Zhu, Yukun, Ryan Kiros, Rich Zemel, Ruslan Salakhutdinov, Raquel Urtasun, Antonio Torralba, and Sanja Fidler. 2015. Aligning books and movies: Towards story-like visual explanations by watching movies and reading books. In *The IEEE International Conference on Computer Vision (ICCV)*, December.

Zouhar, Vilém and Ondřej Bojar. 2024. Quality and quantity of machine translation references for automated metrics.

Zouhar, Vilém, Věra Kloudová, Martin Popel, and Ondřej Bojar. 2023. Evaluating optimal reference translations.

A Translation

A.1 English to French dataset

A.1.1 Correlations

Scatter plots 6, 7, 8, 9, 10, 11 show how well the `lv2` and GV^2 measures correlate between source sentence and HT, MT1 and MT2 sentences on *books, wmt and wilde datasets.*

A.1.2 Absolute values

Figures 12, 21, 22, 13, 14, 15, 16, 17 and 18 show histograms of the senetence-level values of `lv2`, CV and GV^2 across *books, wmt and wilde datasets.* Figures 19 and 20 show the `lv2` histograms on *wilde* and *wmt* after applying filtering based on COMET threshold of the MT.

Figures 24 and 25 show values of CV and GV^2 depending on the COMET threshold for MT translations.

Figure 23 shows the relationship between the COMET score threshold on the *human* translation and the mean `lv2` score of the source sentence and all the translations. We see that in *books, global and wmt*, both the source sentence and the translations are more uniform for high COMET scores. This might suggest a preference of COMET score for uniform surprisal (for example, rooted in training data).

A.1.3 Multiple reference dataset

We experimented also with alternative preprocessing and LMs for estimating the word-level surprisals in the Czech translations of the ORT dataset. The estimates in the main text are computed on untokenized input, i.e. surprisals of punctuation adjacent to a word are summed with that word's surprisal. In Tables 5 and 6, we present the results on tokenized (i.e. punctuation surprisals are considered separately) texts and texts with punctuation removed altogether. We also used an alternative language model (`BUT-FIT/Czech-GPT-2-XL-133k`) to estimate the surprises. See Tables 7, 8, 9 for untok-

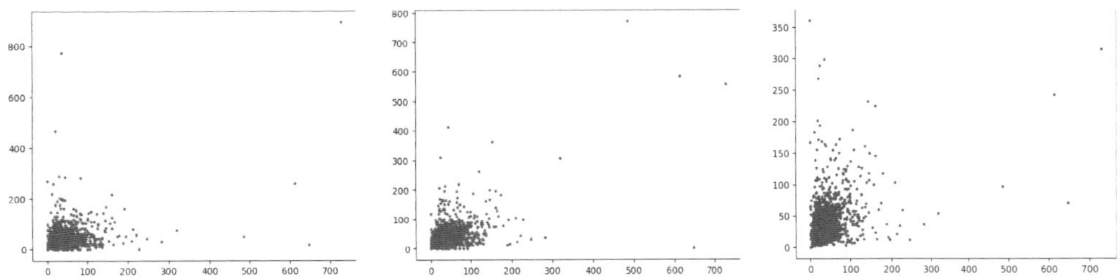

(a) HT (b) MT1 (c) MT2

Figure 6: Scatter plots of `lv2` on *books* dataset between source, and either HT, MT1 or MT2.

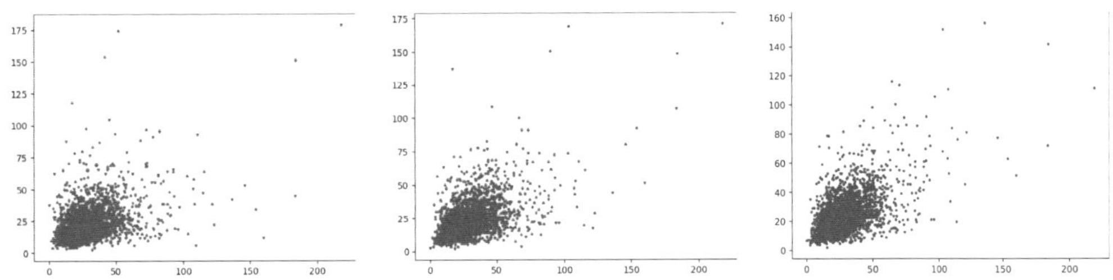

(a) HT (b) MT1 (c) MT2

Figure 7: Scatter plots of `lv2` on *wmt* dataset between source, and either HT, MT1 or MT2.

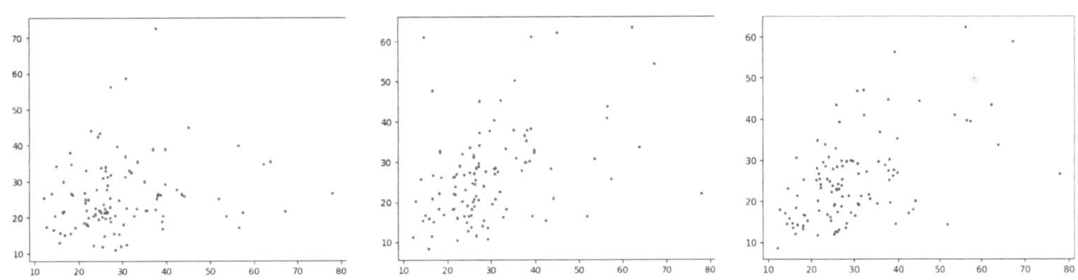

(a) HT (b) MT1 (c) MT2

Figure 8: Scatter plots of `lv2` on *wilde* dataset between source, and either HT, MT1 or MT2.

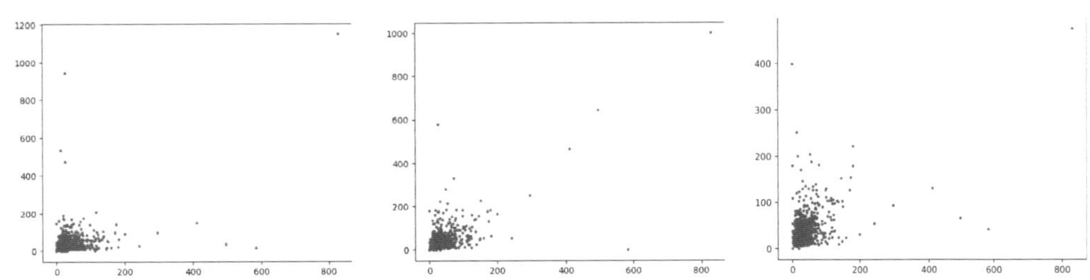

(a) HT (b) MT1 (c) MT2

Figure 9: Scatter plots of GV^2 on *books* dataset between source, and either HT, MT1 or MT2.

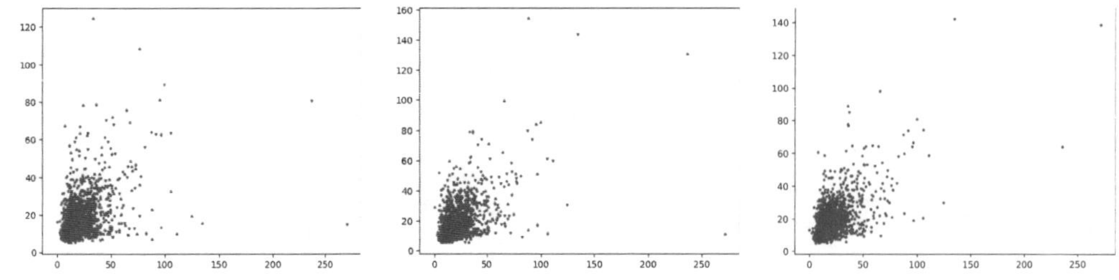

(a) HT (b) MT1 (c) MT2

Figure 10: Scatter plots of GV^2 on *wmt* dataset between source, and either HT, MT1 or MT2.

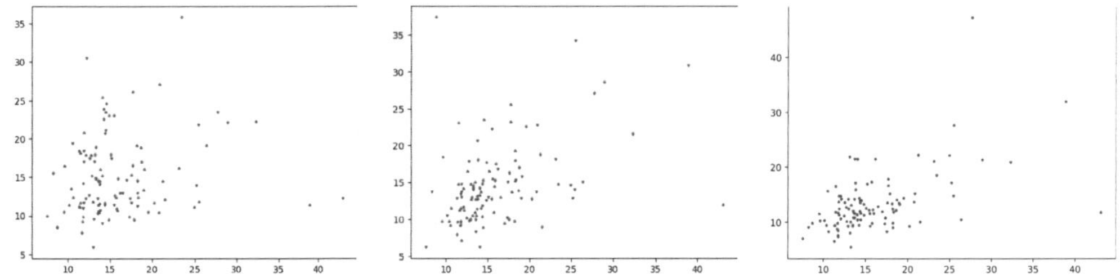

(a) HT (b) MT1 (c) MT2

Figure 11: Scatter plots of GV^2 on *wilde* dataset between source, and either HT, MT1 or MT2.

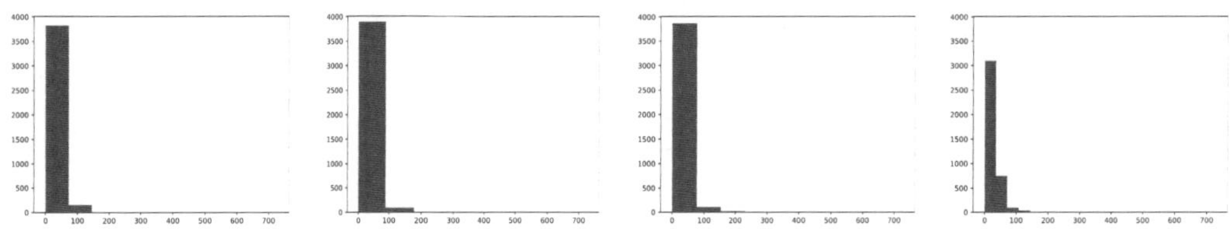

(a) SRC (b) HT (c) MT1 (d) MT2

Figure 12: Histogram of `lv2` on *books* dataset for source, HT, MT1 and MT2.

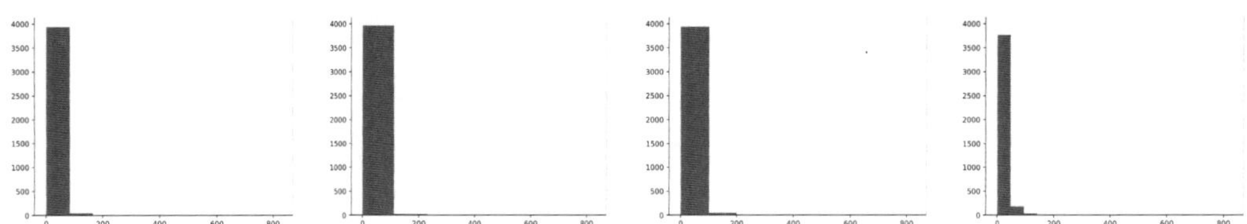

(a) SRC (b) HT (c) MT1 (d) MT2

Figure 13: Histogram of GV^2 on *books* dataset for source, HT, MT1 and MT2.

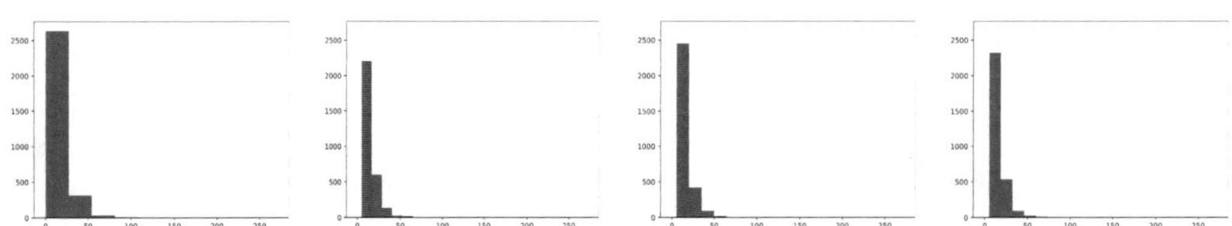

(a) SRC (b) HT (c) MT1 (d) MT2

Figure 14: Histogram of GV^2 on *wmt* dataset for source, HT, MT1 and MT2.

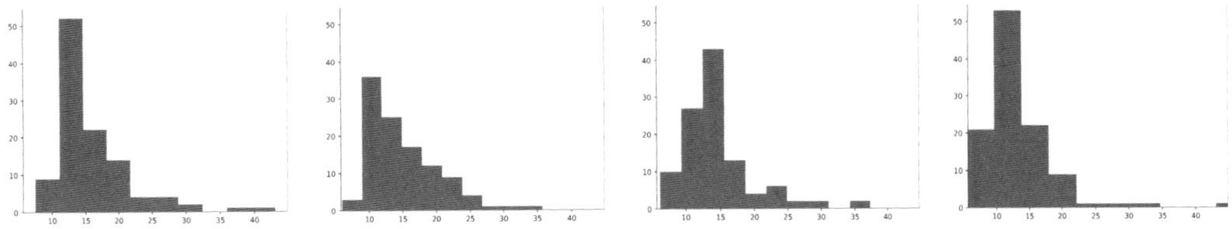

(a) SRC (b) HT (c) MT1 (d) MT2

Figure 15: Histogram of GV^2 on *wilde* datasets for source, HT, MT1 and MT2.

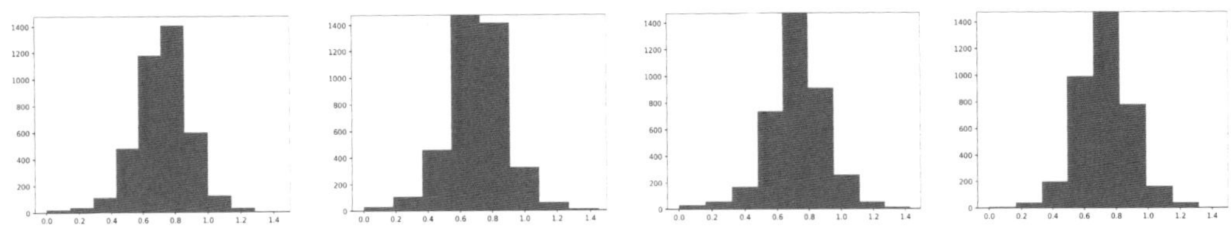

(a) SRC (b) HT (c) MT1 (d) MT2

Figure 16: Histogram of CV on *books* dataset for source, HT, MT1 and MT2.

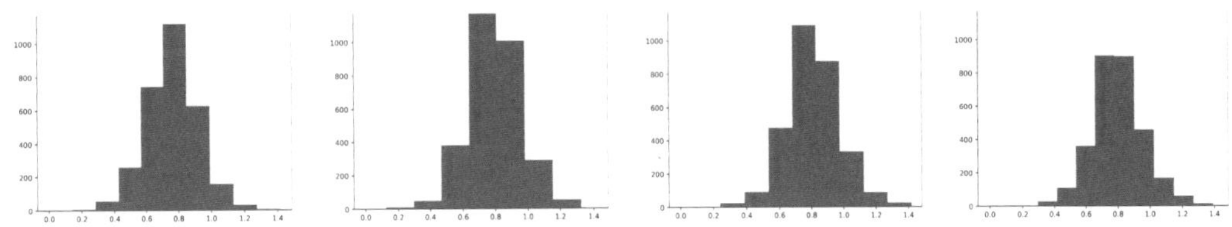

(a) SRC (b) HT (c) MT1 (d) MT2

Figure 17: Histogram of CV on *wmt* dataset for source, HT, MT1 and MT2.

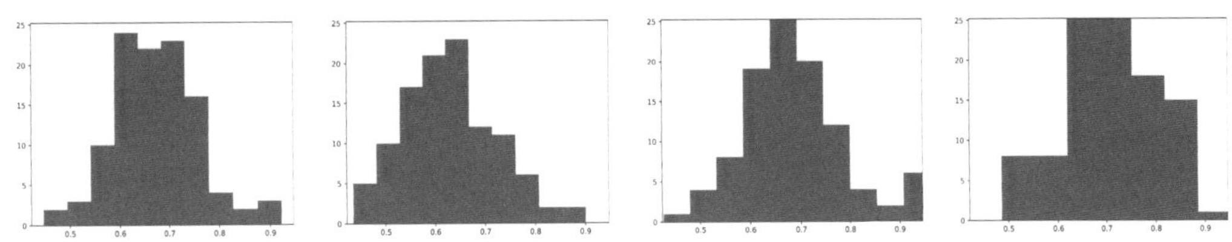

(a) SRC (b) HT (c) MT1 (d) MT2

Figure 18: Histogram of CV on *wilde* datasets for source, HT, MT1 and MT2.

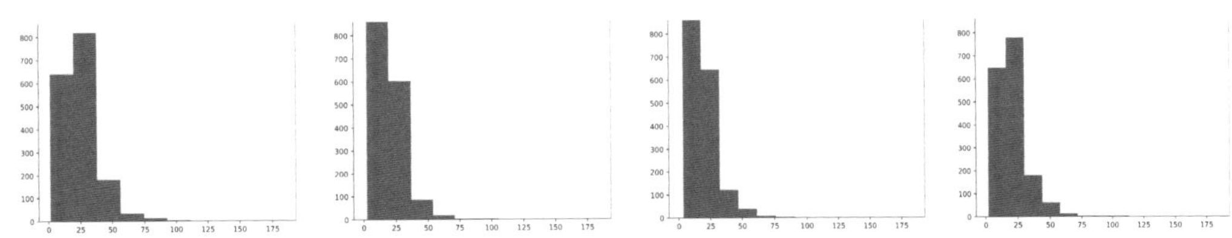

(a) SRC (b) HT (c) MT1 (d) MT2

Figure 19: Histograms of `lv2` on *wmt* dataset for source, HT, MT1 and MT2, after applying COMET threshold, only keeping examples where MT1 COMET score is above 0.88

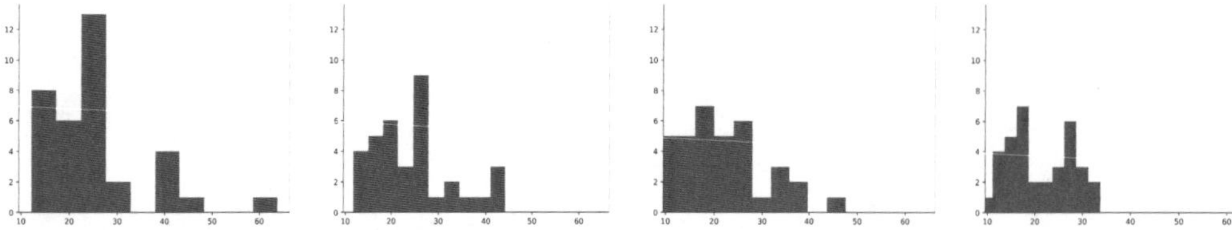

(a) SRC (b) HT (c) MT1 (d) MT2

Figure 20: Histograms of `lv2` on *wilde* dataset for source, HT, MT1 and MT2, after applying COMET threshold, only keeping examples where MT1 COMET score is above 0.72

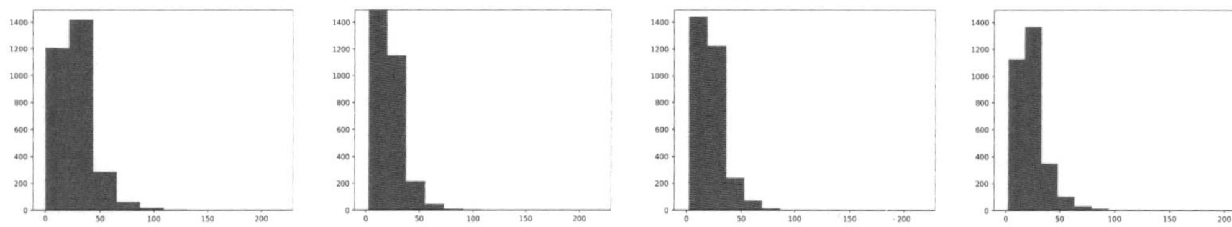

(a) SRC (b) HT (c) MT1 (d) MT2

Figure 21: Histogram of `lv2` on *wmt* dataset for source, HT, MT1 and MT2.

enized, tokenized and punctuation-free results, respectivelly.

Figures 26 and 27 show mean values of CV and GV^2 scores on unfiltered, whole dataset (orange) and dataset containing only examples where COMET score for both `mt` and `mt2` is above 0.88.

metric	src	ref1	ref2	ref3	ref4	mt	mt2
$\mu(s^{0.25})$	1.73	1.52	1.55	1.55	1.51	1.56	1.55
$\rho(s^{0.25})$	0.07	0.08	0.08	0.09	0.08	0.09	0.09
$\mu(s)$	10.36	7.03	7.47	7.46	6.90	7.69	7.48
$\rho(s)$	1.48	1.25	1.28	1.31	1.14	1.39	1.32
$\mu(s^3)$	2814	1211	1444	1372	1155	1525	1390
$\rho(s^3)$	1316	837	859	896	768	893	959
$\mu(gini)$	0.32	0.39	0.38	0.38	0.39	0.38	0.38
$\rho(gini)$	0.05	0.05	0.06	0.05	0.05	0.05	0.05
$\mu(CV)$	0.60	0.73	0.73	0.71	0.74	0.72	0.71
$\rho(CV)$	0.10	0.13	0.13	0.12	0.13	0.13	0.13
$\mu(LV^2)$	72.4	44.8	48.6	47.0	44.4	47.8	49.4
$\rho(LV^2)$	29.5	22.0	23.4	22.5	21.1	21.2	26.7
$\mu(GV^2)$	41.8	27.9	31.4	30.0	27.3	32.5	30.3
$\rho(GV^2)$	17.2	13.5	14.2	14.8	13.1	15.0	16.1
$\mu(GV^2_{glob})$	27.9	27.9	31.4	30.0	27.3	32.7	30.4
$\rho(GV^2_{glob})$	13.1	13.1	14.4	15.0	12.6	15.6	16.4

Table 5: Mean values and standard deviations of sentenece-level uniformity measures for source, two machine translations and the three human reference sets. The texts **are** tokenized for the surprisal estimation, thus the estimates for punctuation are considered separately in the uniformity measures' calculations.

metric	src	ref1	ref2	ref3	ref4	mt	mt2
$\mu(s^{0.25})$	1.73	1.48	1.50	1.51	1.47	1.52	1.51
$\rho(s^{0.25})$	0.07	0.09	0.09	0.09	0.09	0.09	0.10
$\mu(s)$	10.36	6.48	6.74	6.89	6.35	6.96	6.97
$\rho(s)$	1.48	1.37	1.33	1.37	1.27	1.47	1.49
$\mu(s^3)$	2814	1156	1214	1264	1097	1249	1360
$\rho(s^3)$	1316	948	923	947	867	897	1097
$\mu(gini)$	0.32	0.40	0.39	0.39	0.41	0.39	0.40
$\rho(gini)$	0.05	0.06	0.06	0.06	0.05	0.06	0.06
$\mu(CV)$	0.60	0.79	0.76	0.76	0.80	0.75	0.77
$\rho(CV)$	0.10	0.15	0.15	0.14	0.14	0.14	0.15
$\mu(LV^2)$	72.4	42.2	43.5	44.4	41.4	42.8	48.3
$\rho(LV^2)$	29.5	25.7	26.2	25.1	24.1	23.7	30.7
$\mu(GV^2)$	41.8	28.2	28.6	29.5	27.5	29.0	31.4
$\rho(GV^2)$	17.2	16.4	16.4	16.5	15.9	16.5	19.5
$\mu(GV^2\_glob)$	28.1	28.1	28.6	29.6	27.4	29.1	31.6
$\rho(GV^2\_glob)$	16.0	16.0	16.4	16.8	15.3	16.9	20.0

Table 6: Mean values and standard deviations of sentenece-level uniformity measures for source, two machine translations and the three human reference sets. The surprisal estimates for punctuation are discarded for the uniformity measures' calculation.

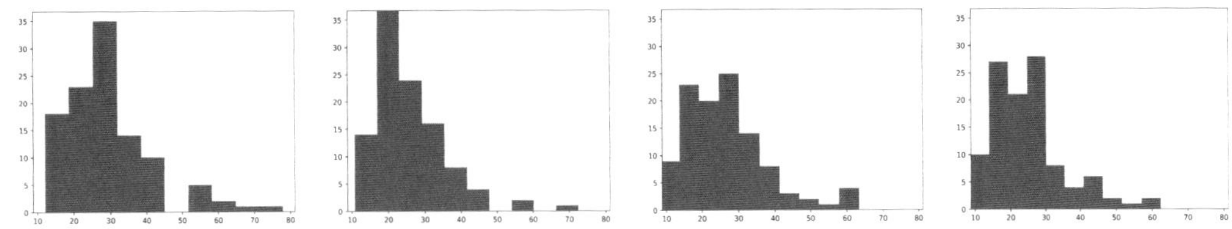

(a) SRC (b) HT (c) MT1 (d) MT2

Figure 22: Histogram of `lv2` on *wilde* dataset for source, HT, MT1 and MT2.

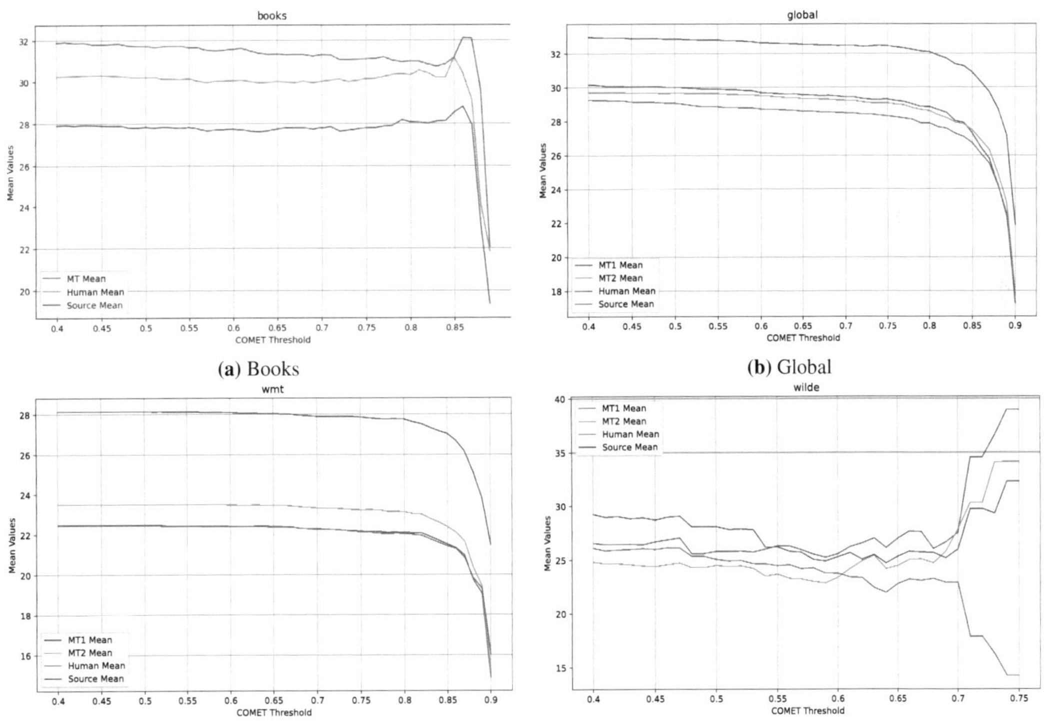

(a) Books (b) Global (c) WMT (d) Wilde

Figure 23: Relationship between COMET scores of the HT and the `lv2` measure.

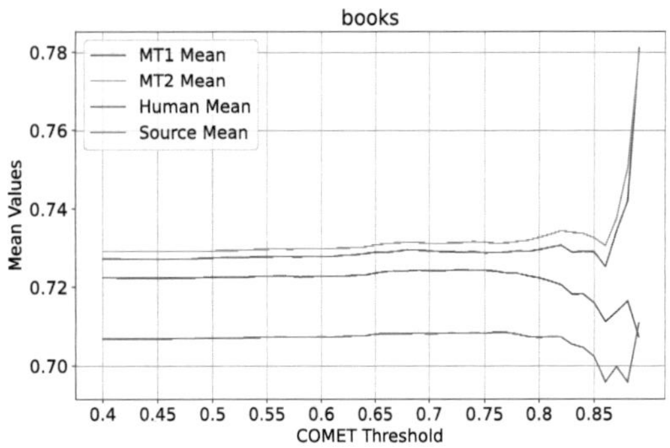

(a) Books

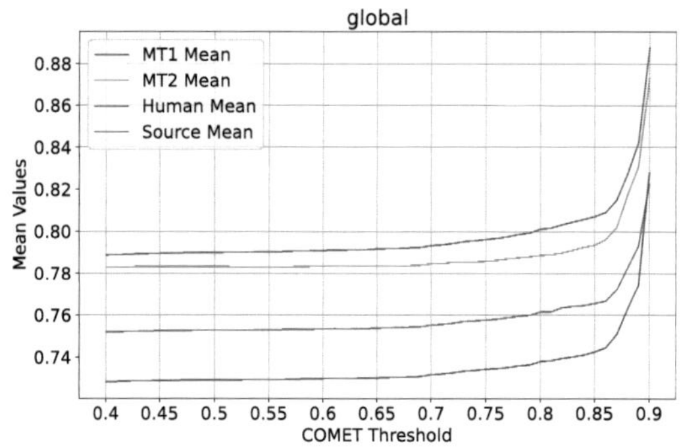

(b) Global

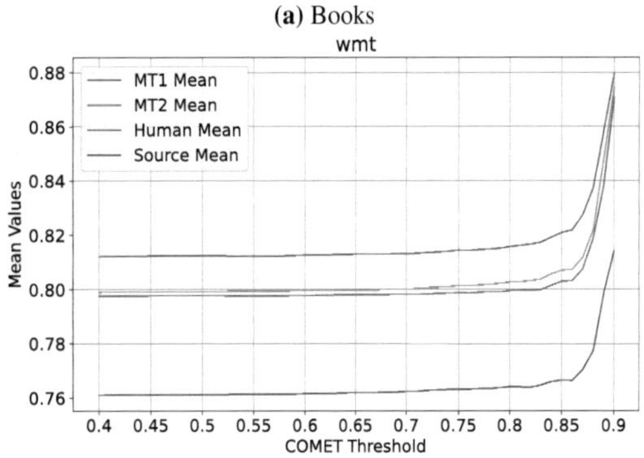

(c) WMT

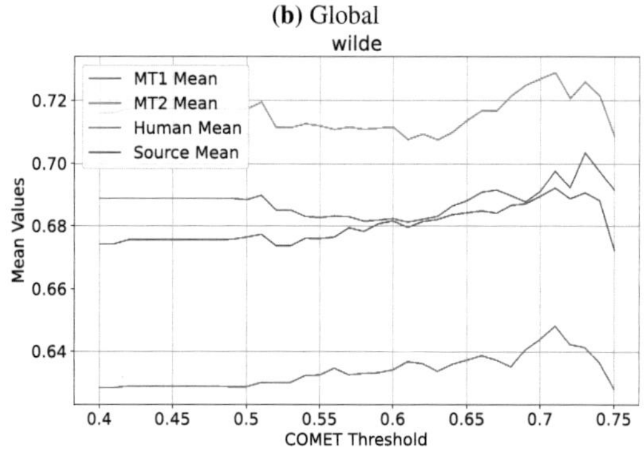

(d) Wilde

Figure 24: Relationship between COMET scores of the MT and the CV measure. As a proxy of translation quality, we use COMET score threshold to filter out low-quality translations.

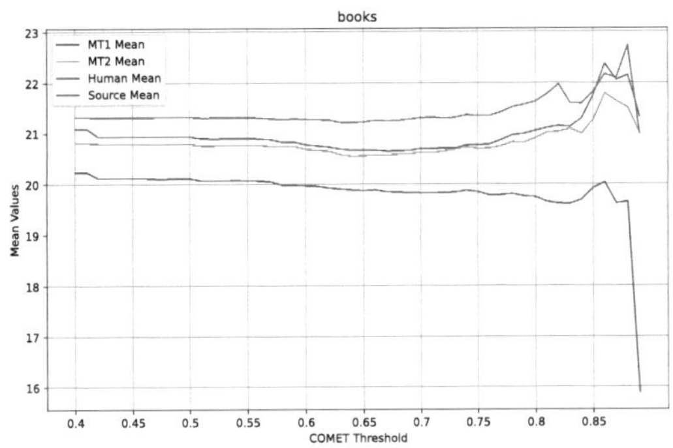

(b) Books

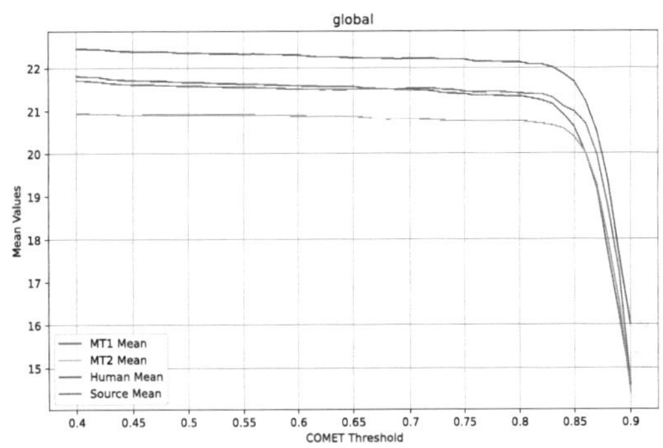

(a) Global

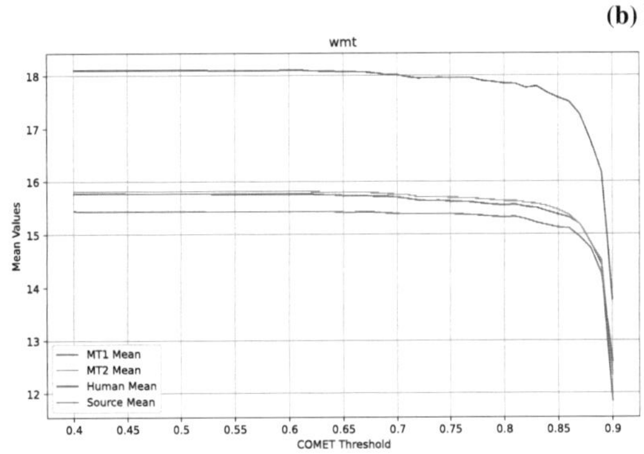

(c) WMT

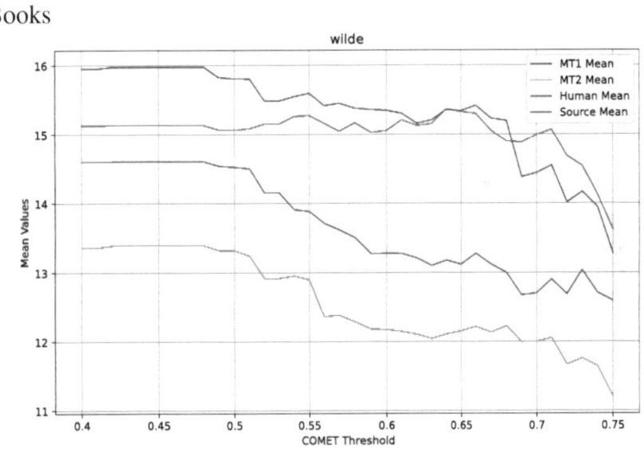

(d) Wilde

Figure 25: Relationship between COMET scores of the MT and the GV^2 measure. As a proxy of translation quality, we use COMET score threshold to filter out low-quality translations.

metric	src	ref1	ref2	ref3	ref4	mt	mt2
$\mu(s^{0.25})$	1.72	1.35	1.37	1.39	1.33	1.39	1.39
$\rho(s^{0.25})$	0.08	0.10	0.09	0.10	0.09	0.11	0.10
$\mu(s)$	10.21	4.70	4.96	5.25	4.55	5.24	5.30
$\rho(s)$	1.62	1.01	1.02	1.09	0.94	1.26	1.23
$\mu(s^3)$	2797	417	483	565	397	540	615
$\rho(s^3)$	1497	355	383	425	322	460	553
$\mu(gini)$	0.33	0.42	0.42	0.42	0.43	0.42	0.43
$\rho(gini)$	0.05	0.06	0.06	0.06	0.06	0.06	0.06
$\mu(CV)$	0.62	0.80	0.79	0.79	0.82	0.77	0.80
$\rho(CV)$	0.11	0.15	0.15	0.15	0.14	0.14	0.15
$\mu(LV^2)$	70.6	26.6	29.9	32.0	26.5	30.2	34.7
$\rho(LV^2)$	30.4	15.4	16.8	16.3	14.7	16.5	20.4
$\mu(GV^2)$	42.0	14.8	16.3	17.9	14.5	17.2	19.0
$\rho(GV^2)$	18.7	7.9	8.7	9.2	7.5	9.8	11.5
$\mu(GV^2\_glob)$	14.8	14.8	16.3	18.1	14.5	17.3	19.2
$\rho(GV^2\_glob)$	7.6	7.6	8.7	9.5	7.0	10.1	11.9

Table 7: Mean values and standard deviations of sentenece-level uniformity measures for source, two machine translations and the three human reference sets. The texts are not tokenized for the surprisal estimation, thus the estimates for punctuation are often summed up with the adjacent words in the calculations of the uniformity metrics. The surprisals are calculated by `BUT-FIT/Czech-GPT-2-XL-133k` model.

metric	src	ref1	ref2	ref3	ref4	mt	mt2
$\mu(s^{0.25})$	1.73	1.33	1.36	1.36	1.32	1.38	1.37
$\rho(s^{0.25})$	0.07	0.09	0.09	0.09	0.09	0.10	0.10
$\mu(s)$	10.36	4.45	4.77	4.83	4.32	5.06	4.92
$\rho(s)$	1.48	0.89	0.91	0.95	0.82	1.21	1.09
$\mu(s^3)$	2814	356	441	439	336	518	499
$\rho(s^3)$	1316	300	325	346	266	494	461
$\mu(gini)$	0.32	0.43	0.43	0.42	0.44	0.42	0.43
$\rho(gini)$	0.05	0.06	0.06	0.06	0.06	0.06	0.06
$\mu(CV)$	0.60	0.80	0.81	0.79	0.82	0.79	0.80
$\rho(CV)$	0.10	0.14	0.15	0.14	0.14	0.14	0.16
$\mu(LV^2)$	72.4	24.6	27.3	27.3	24.5	28.4	30.7
$\rho(LV^2)$	29.5	12.5	13.8	13.4	11.9	15.5	17.9
$\mu(GV^2)$	41.8	13.4	15.7	15.4	13.2	17.3	17.0
$\rho(GV^2)$	17.2	6.7	7.6	7.8	6.1	10.6	10.3
$\mu(GV^2\_glob)$	13.4	13.4	15.7	15.5	13.2	17.5	17.1
$\rho(GV^2\_glob)$	6.5	6.5	7.7	7.9	5.8	11.2	10.6

Table 8: Mean values and standard deviations of sentence-level uniformity measures for source, two machine translations and the three human reference sets. The surprisals are calculated by `BUT-FIT/Czech-GPT-2-XL-133k` model. The texts **are** tokenized for the surprisal estimation, thus the estimates for punctuation are considered separately in the uniformity measures' calculations.

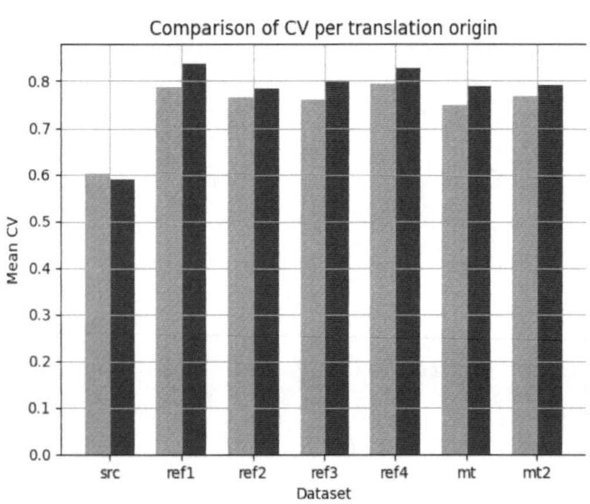

Figure 26: Difference of CV scores between all (orange) and high-quality (green) MT translations.

metric	src	ref1	ref2	ref3	ref4	mt	mt2
$\mu(s^{0.25})$	1.73	1.33	1.35	1.36	1.31	1.37	1.37
$\rho(s^{0.25})$	0.07	0.10	0.09	0.10	0.09	0.11	0.10
$\mu(s)$	10.36	4.52	4.77	4.91	4.38	5.07	5.05
$\rho(s)$	1.48	0.96	0.97	1.01	0.90	1.22	1.17
$\mu(s^3)$	2814	380	433	461	359	488	537
$\rho(s^3)$	1316	342	359	385	304	416	512
$\mu(gini)$	0.32	0.43	0.43	0.42	0.44	0.42	0.43
$\rho(gini)$	0.05	0.06	0.07	0.06	0.06	0.06	0.06
$\mu(CV)$	0.60	0.81	0.80	0.79	0.83	0.78	0.81
$\rho(CV)$	0.10	0.15	0.15	0.15	0.14	0.14	0.16
$\mu(LV^2)$	72.4	25.1	27.9	28.0	25.1	28.2	32.1
$\rho(LV^2)$	29.5	14.6	16.2	14.8	13.9	15.1	20.3
$\mu(GV^2)$	41.8	14.0	15.3	15.7	13.8	16.2	17.8
$\rho(GV^2)$	17.2	7.6	8.2	8.4	7.0	8.9	11.2
$\mu(GV^2\_glob)$	14.0	14.0	15.3	15.8	13.8	16.4	18.0
$\rho(GV^2\_glob)$	7.3	7.3	8.2	8.5	6.6	9.3	11.5

Table 9: Mean values and standard deviations of sentence-level uniformity measures for source, two machine translations and the three human reference sets. The surprisals are calculated by `BUT-FIT/Czech-GPT-2-XL-133k` model. The surprisal estimates for punctuation are discarded for the uniformity measures' calculation.

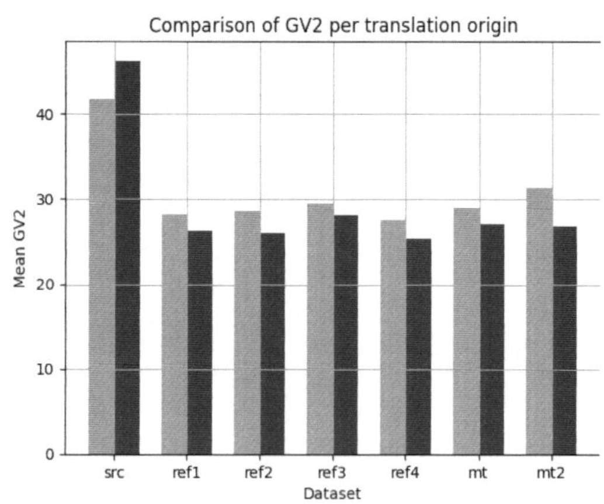

Figure 27: Difference of GV^2 scores between all (orange) and high-quality (green) MT translations.

Impact of translation workflows with and without MT on textual characteristics in literary translation

Joke Daems, Paola Ruffo, and Lieve Macken
LT3, Language and Translation Technology Team
Ghent University
Belgium
{firstname.lastname}@ugent.be

Abstract

The use of machine translation is increasingly being explored for the translation of literary texts, but there is still a lot of uncertainty about the optimal translation workflow in these scenarios. While overall quality is quite good, certain textual characteristics can be different in a human translated text and a text produced by means of machine translation post-editing, which has been shown to potentially have an impact on reader perceptions and experience as well. In this study, we look at textual characteristics from short story translations from B.J. Novak's *One more thing* into Dutch. Twenty-three professional literary translators translated three short stories, in three different conditions: using Word, using the classic CAT tool Trados, and using a machine translation post-editing platform specifically designed for literary translation. We look at overall text characteristics (sentence length, type-token ratio, stylistic differences) to establish whether translation workflow has an impact on these features, and whether the three workflows lead to very different final translations or not.

1 Introduction

While originally an outrageous or at least unorthodox idea, the concept of using technology and even machine translation for literary texts has gained ground in recent years. This is evidenced by the existence of works specifically dedicated to technology and creative-text translation (Hadley et al., 2022), the existence of a Literary MT Workshop (dating back to 2019) or the present workshop on Creative-text Translation and Technology at EAMT 2024.

For certain sentences, even raw MT output is seen as comparable to human translation (Toral & Way, 2018), and post-editing NMT output has been shown to be much faster than from-scratch translation for certain language combinations (Terribile, 2023), making it a potentially fruitful way of working, even for literary texts. While time gains are very high for a language combination like English-French, post-editing is actually slower for English-Swedish (Terribile, 2023).

However, additional factors that need to be taken into account are the concerns from literary translators themselves (Daems, 2022; Ruffo, 2021) and the impact of technology-mediated literary translation on a reader's experience (Guerberof-Arenas & Toral, 2020). As part of the broader DUAL-T project[1], which aims to include literary translators' voices in the development of technology-mediated literary translation, this study explores the impact of three different conditions with different degrees of technological support on textual characteristics, which are assumed to influence reader perceptions of a final text.

We continue by exploring some relevant concepts in the field of MT for literary texts and related work on textual features and reader experiences, followed by our research methodology, analysis and results, and we end with conclusions and plans for future work.

2 Related research

An important consideration when using MT for literary text translation, is that MT has been shown to lead to a decrease in lexical richness

[1] https://www.ugent.be/en/research/explorer/eu-trackrecord/heu/heu-msca/dualt.htm

Proceedings of the 1st Workshop on Creative-text Translation and Technology, pages 57–64
June 27, 2024 ©2024 European Association for Machine Translation

(Vanmassenhove et al., 2019). Even after post-editing, the effects of the MT seem to linger, with post-edited texts having lower lexical variety and density than human translations, and having more interference from the source language (Toral, 2019).

In the context of literary machine translation specifically, research has shown that MT systems (both Google Translate and DeepL) produce texts that are lexically less diverse than human translations, and that they have lower lexical and semantic cohesion (Webster et al., 2020). The authors also calculated stylistic differences using Burrows' Delta and found that the styles of Google Translate and DeepL were quite similar, whereas the distance between both MT systems and the human translations was much greater (Webster et al., 2020). Even in a post-editing context, where a professional literary translator is actively requested to keep his own typical translator style, certain words he normally would avoid are still maintained from the MT suggestions (Winters & Kenny, 2023).

Subsequent research into reading experiences found that differences between human translations, machine translations and post-edited texts led to differences in narrative engagement, with human translations generally being rated higher (Guerberof-Arenas & Toral, 2024). However, the authors also found some surprising differences between different languages, with Catalan readers preferring human translations and Dutch readers preferring to read a text in the English source, or the post-edited version, potentially precisely *because* it remains closer to the source (Guerberof-Arenas & Toral, 2024).

These studies suggest that it is crucial to explore textual features of translations produced in different conditions, in order to (in future) explore the influence on translators style and to predict the effects on reading experiences for different kinds of readers.

3 Methodology

The goal of this study was to explore the impact of translation workflow on final text characteristics. Different translation workflows were simulated by means of three possible translation conditions: Microsoft Word without specific translation technology support, Trados Studio 2022 with a relevant translation memory and termbase, and a proprietary MTPE platform. The main textual features we wanted to explore were:

- **Average sentence length and differences in sentence alignment** between source text and translations across conditions. We hypothesized that translators would stay closer to the source text structure and text length, particularly in the MTPE condition (Toral, 2019; Webster et al., 2020), and that they would feel less constrained in the Word condition (Daems, 2022).
- **Lexical diversity** for different conditions. We hypothesized that the more technology-driven workflows would lead to lexically less diverse translations across participants (Guerberof-Arenas & Toral, 2024; Vanmassenhove et al., 2019; Webster et al., 2020).
- **Stylometric differences** between conditions and between the official human translation or MT translation and the corresponding post-edited version. We hypothesized that there would be fewer differences between MTPE texts than between the texts in the Word condition, given the expected interference from the MT output (Toral, 2019) and that MTPE texts would cluster close together with the original MT output, based on earlier findings that using MT can lead to interference with a typical translator's style (Winters & Kenny, 2023).

3.1 Participants

A total of 23 professional English-Dutch translators were recruited for this study via connections established during earlier studies in this field and professional translator associations in Flanders and the Netherlands. Participants were paid 250 euros for their participation (a session lasted 4-5 hours, so participants received 50-60 euros per hour) and received reimbursement of their travel costs.

A diverse set of participants was recruited, with an average age of 48 and an average of 12 years of literary translation experience. Looking at age bands per 10 years, six participants belonged to the youngest age range (26-35) and three participants to the oldest age range (66-75). Participants had between one year and 43 years of literary translation experience.

With regards to technology use, eight participants indicated they had experience working with

CAT tools (four indicated they also used them for literary translation), and eight participants indicated they used post-editing (four indicated they also used it for literary translation).

3.2 Text selection & data preparation

Three short stories were selected from the 2014 short story collection *One More Thing* by B. J. Novak. The selection was driven by a mix of practical factors, such as the fact that the stories were short enough to be translated in one sitting while still being a self-contained piece of narrative, results of readability analyses, and the fact that the humorous and sarcastic nature of the stories could offer some challenges to the translators. The selected texts are titled *Rome* (321 words, 30 sentences, 10.7 words per sentence on average words per sentence), *The Beautiful Girl in the Bookstore* (353 words, 27 sentences, 13.07 average words per sentence), and *They Kept Driving Faster and Outran the Rain* (303 words, 30 sentences, 10.1 average words per sentence). We include a snippet from each text below (Fragments 1-3) to show some of the typical difficulties in the texts.

> He loved saying "Rome" like that. "Head into Rome," "swing by Rome." It was just the nearest place to them. How cool was that! Rome, the city of legends, of conquerors, of history, of myth—this was where he bought *batteries*! The place that people saved up to visit their whole lives: for him, this really was simply the place where he might fill up on gas one day and where the next day he'd have to know the right shop to pick up flowers for his wife to thank her for making dinner—with ingredients he had also picked up in Rome. Rome! That's all Rome was to him! Nothing special at all!

Fragment 1: Snippet from the story *Rome,* containing examples of multi-word expressions, repetition, contrast, and complex syntactic structures.

> There was a magnifying glass built out of a knotted clunk of iron with a foggy lens that magically made even the most serious face, her boyfriend's face, for example, evaporate into a vague and bloated and goofy smile that never failed to make her laugh.
> Things like that.
> "How good does this book smell," she said, pulling a paperback from a shelf. "Like dust on a bottle of vanilla."

Fragment 2: Snippet from the story *The Beautiful Girl in the Bookstore,* containing examples of compound nominals, complex syntactic structures, metaphor and original images.

> *"I love the fauna here at the hotel."*
> *"Wait, what's fauna?"*
> *"Plants, flowers, right?"*
> *"Right, but 'flora* and *fauna.' Isn't flora flowers?"*
> *"Then what's fauna?"*
> *"Don't know. Let's look it up later."*
> *"K."*
> *"K."*

Fragment 3: Snippet from the story *They Kept Driving Faster and Outran the Rain,* containing examples of dialogue and colloquial language use.

Another reason for selecting this collection was that it has been translated into Dutch (*Onverzameld Werk*, translated by Jevgenia Lodewijks, Lydia Meeder, and Maarten van der Werf), so it was possible to create a translation memory and termbase from this material. The translation memory contained the entire collection in English and Dutch, with the exception of the three short stories selected for the study. To generate the termbase, Sketch Engine was used to automatically extract key terms from the entire collection, in this case *including* the three short stories to ensure that at least some terms would be recognized in the texts during translation. As non-commercial research studies form an exception to copyright, no formal permission was sought. We did ensure that none of the material was made public in any way. All participants completed the experiment on the researcher's device, which had a local copy of the translation memory. The MTPE platform connects to an MT system via API to ensure that no data is shared with the company.

3.3 Experimental setup

Participants read an information letter and signed an informed consent form. They then read a translation brief providing some background information on the short story collection and they were instructed to provide a final translation of publishable quality (to the best of their ability in the respective conditions). Participants completed a survey about their professional background and experience with technology.

All participants translated each of the three texts and worked in each of the three translation conditions. While the Microsoft Word condition was always the first condition, the order of the other conditions (Trados and the MTPE platform) was mixed across participants to control for task order effects. Word was used as a baseline, since it is the workflow most literary translators are familiar with, and it allowed us to have less workflow-text combinations to work with. Text order was also mixed and balanced so that each combination of text and condition appeared a similar number of times. During translation, translators were allowed to use online resources. The translation process was logged using keystroke logging (Inputlog 8.0) and screen recording (OBS Studio 29.1.3).

At the end of the session, participants received a survey where they could rank the different translation workflows and they also took part in an in-depth interview to explore their attitudes and experiences in more detail. The process measure analyses and interview data form the focus of other publications within the broader DUAL-T project (currently under review).

3.4 Data processing

All the produced translations were saved as simple text files for further processing. Texts were first split into sentences and tokenized using Stanza (Qi et al., 2020) then manually aligned for comparison across texts. A couple of different textual features were studied:

Average sentence length: A custom Python script was used to calculate and compare the average sentence length across conditions.

Alignment types: Based on the manual sentence alignment, we could determine how frequently participants diverged from the source text structures and decided to split or merge sentences.

Lexical diversity: Moving average TTR was calculated with the default window size of 50 words, using the lexical-diversity package[2] in Python.

Stylometric differences: The stylo package in R (Eder et al., 2016) was used to calculate classic Delta distances (Burrows, 2002) between texts and explore stylometric differences across texts and conditions. First, stylo generates a list of the most frequent words (MFW) in the whole corpus (the number of words is determined by the user). Then, the frequency of each of those words is checked for each text in the corpus. Burrow's Delta uses *z-scores* (normalized word frequencies) to calculate how big the difference is between the word use in a given text and the corpus as a whole. While this seems like a relatively simplistic approach, the method has proven very successful in authorship attribution, showing that texts with similar scores are generally written by the same author. We created a mini corpus for each source text, containing all translations of that text, including the reference human translation and the machine translation. Given that the words used are very different in each source text, we did not perform the analysis on the corpus as a whole (all translations would simply cluster together per source text). We used stylo to create a bootstrap consensus tree using the 100-500 most frequent words (with 100-word increments). This means that stylo performs a cluster analysis (calculating Burrow's Delta and showing how close different translations cluster together based on those values) for the 100 MFW, 200 MFW, 300 MFW, 400 MFW, and 500 MFW and then combines the results of those cluster analyses to generate the consensus tree (texts that cluster together for at least 50% of the cluster analyses will cluster together in the consensus tree).

4 Results

4.1 Average sentence length and alignment types

Table 1 shows the difference in number of words, sentences and average sentence length for the original source texts, the MT version and the human reference translation. From this, we can see that MT generally stays closer to the source text length than the reference human translator does, and that the number of sentences is exactly the same. A human translator introduces a bit more variability, although the difference in number of sentences is minimal. Average sentence length was lower in the human reference translation for text 1, but higher for text 2 and 3.

TEXT	words	sentences	avg. sentence length
ST1	321	30	10.70
MT1	320	30	10.67
REF1	292	29	10.07
ST2	353	27	13.07
MT2	350	27	12.96
REF2	390	28	13.93
ST3	303	30	10.10
MT3	305	30	10.17
REF3	323	30	10.77

Table 1: Number of words, sentences, and average sentence length for the original source text, machine translation, and reference human translation for each text.

[2] https://pypi.org/project/lexical-diversity/

When we compare this to the average sentence length and ranges for the texts produced by the participants in the different conditions (Table 2), we actually do not see that much difference between the different conditions for each text. Even when considering individual variability across participants by looking at the range between the lowest and highest possible average sentence length, the Word condition does not lead to the greatest variability (as expected), with the exception of text 3, where the range of scores is greater than that in the Trados and MTPE conditions.

CONDITION & TEXT	mean	min	max
MTPE 1	10.55	9.5	11.76
Trados 1	10.53	9.9	11.47
Word 1	10.68	10.1	11.48
MTPE 2	13.25	12.59	13.96
Trados 2	13.32	12.52	14.07
Word 2	13.12	12.48	13.52
MTPE 3	10.48	10.17	10.93
Trados 3	10.38	10.03	10.8
Word 3	10.45	9.97	11.13

Table 2: Descriptive statistics for the average sentence length for the different conditions and texts.

Like they were in the reference translation, differences in alignment are quite rare in the corpus we collected as well. For text one, there were four instances of alignment changes in the MTPE condition, one in Trados, and two in Word. For text two, there was only one instance of alignment change in the MTPE condition, and one in the Word condition. Text three elicited five alignment changes in total, three in the Trados condition and two in the Word condition. While we hypothesized that the MTPE and Trados environments would create more constraints for literary translators by forcing them to translate on a sentence by sentence level, these numbers show that condition did not obviously limit or encourage changes in sentence alignment between source and target.

4.2 Lexical diversity

The expectation based on previous research was that type-token ratio would be much higher for the Word and Trados conditions compared to the MTPE condition, as MTPE texts have been shown to be lexically less diverse. Based on the average MATTR scores across participants, however (Figure 1), this hypothesis cannot be confirmed.

For text 1 and 2, MTPE is actually the condition with the greatest lexical diversity, and for text 3, the differences between MTPE and Word (the condition with the expected greatest diversity) are minimal. Scores for raw MT output are, perhaps surprisingly, also quite high.

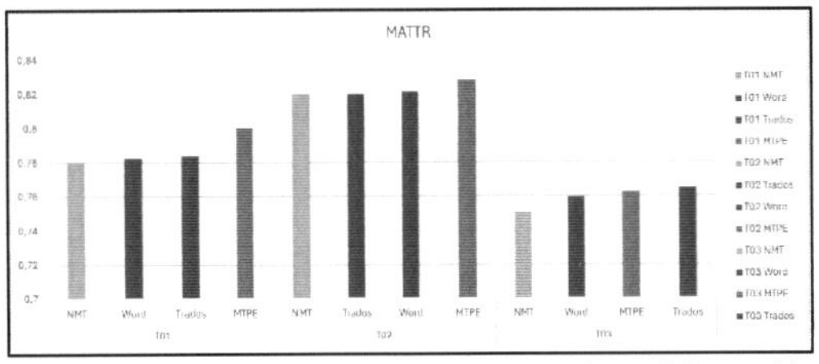

Figure 1: average MATTR for each text and condition, with the MT output as a reference score.

Looking at individual participant scores, we found there are three participants who scored lower on lexical diversity than the raw MT output for text 1 (one in the Trados and two in the Word condition), seven participants for text 2 (two in the MTPE condition, three in the Trados condition, and two in the Word condition), and one for text 3 (in the Trados condition). This shows that post-editing or even regular human translation does not automatically lead to a greater level of lexical diversity.

4.3 Stylometric differences

Figures 2-4 depict the bootstrap consensus tree for each text. In all three, we can see a clear cluster around the machine translation, which exclusively contains translations produced in the MTPE condition (with the exception of one Word translation for text 2). This means that there does seem to be some stylometric similarity between the MT output and a majority of MTPE texts. On the other hand, there are still MTPE translations that appear as part of a mixed cluster (together with Trados and Word conditions) or in isolation, indicating that MT output does not always determine the stylistic outcome of the final MTPE product. The human reference translation is stylistically closest to a translation from the Word or Trados condition, but never to a translation from the MTPE condition.

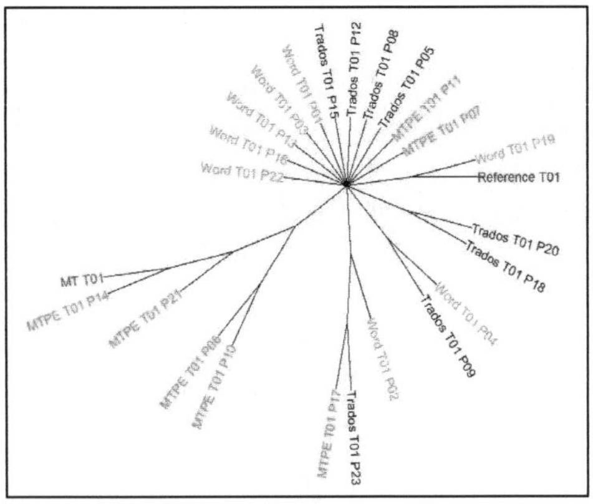

Figure 2: Bootstrap consensus tree for text 1. 100-500 most frequent words without culling, Classic Delta distance Consensus 0.5.

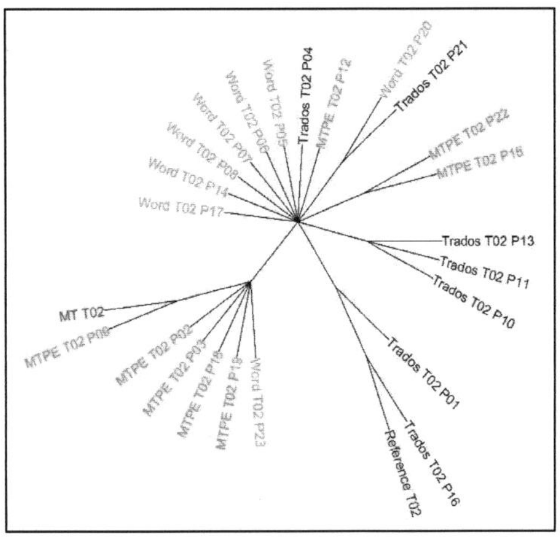

Figure 3: Bootstrap consensus tree for text 2. 100-500 most frequent words without culling, Classic Delta distance Consensus 0.5.

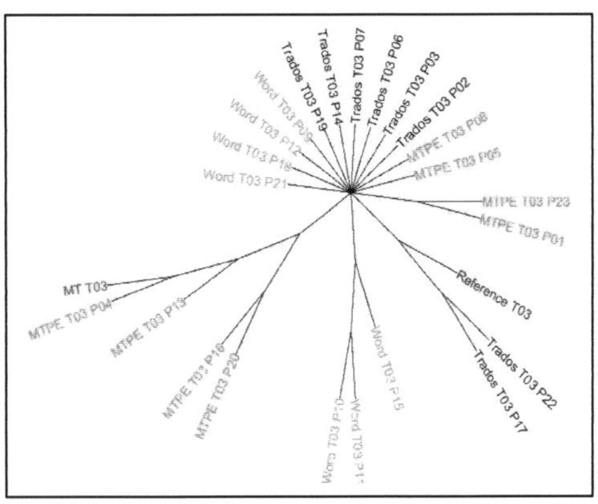

Figure 4: Bootstrap consensus tree for text 3. 100-500 most frequent words without culling, Classic Delta distance Consensus 0.5.

5 Discussion and Conclusions

The main goal of this exploratory study was to establish the impact of translation workflow on textual differences. We compared the translations produced by professional literary translators in three conditions: using Microsoft Word, using Trados, and using a proprietary MTPE tool. The hypothesis was that translations produced in Word would showcase the most individuality and divergence from the source text as the blank page does not offer specific constraints, whereas the MTPE was expected to remain closest to source and/or MT output as it offers the MT output as a starting point. Trados was expected to lead to some constraints (particularly by forcing translators to work on a segment level), but fewer than the MTPE workflow (as there was no translation to start from here).

We compared average sentence length and changes in sentence alignment, lexical diversity, and stylometric differences. Average sentence length did not seem to differ remarkably across conditions. Earlier research on sentence patterns in English and Dutch showed that, in contrast with academic texts, newspaper articles, and leaflets, sentence length for short stories can actually be similar in both languages (Tavecchio, 2010). The present study shows that the condition in which the text was produced does not change this. Changes in sentence alignment were also relatively rare, and occurred in all three conditions, contrary to expectations that they would be most frequent in the Word condition. Based on previous research, we expected MTPE to be less lexically diverse than translations in other conditions, but this could not be confirmed either (on the contrary, MTPE was the most lexically diverse for 2/3 texts). Stylometric analysis based on Burrow's Delta (2002) did show some similarities between MT output and a majority of translations produced in the MTPE condition, indicating that there is some similarity in their word use.

The analysis presented in this paper is a preliminary analysis of textual features in our dataset that contradicts some core assumptions about the 'homogenisation' of MTPE texts, and at the same time encourages additional exploration of the data. For future work, we aim to conduct more extensive analyses on this data, e.g., by exploring if translation workflow influences different metrics of syntactic equivalence (Vanroy et al., 2021). As Winters and Kenny suggest, studies like this "usually branch into richer qualitative analyses on the basis of their initial quantitative findings" (2023, p. 70). This is precisely what we aim to do. We are currently annotating all texts on the basis of units of creative potential and creative shifts (Guerberof-Arenas & Toral, 2022), multi-word units (Colson, 2019), and translation relations (Zhai et al., 2018) in order to get a more in-depth understanding of translation choices and how they are (not) mediated by the different workflows.

Acknowledgements

This project has received funding from the European Union's Horizon Europe (HORIZON) research and innovation programme under the Marie Skłodowska-Curie grant agreement No 101062428.

References

Burrows, J. (2002). 'Delta': A Measure of Stylistic Difference and a Guide to Likely Authorship. *Literary and Linguistic Computing*, *17*(3), 267–287. https://doi.org/10.1093/llc/17.3.267

Colson, J.-P. (2019). Multi-word Units in Machine Translation: Why the Tip of the Iceberg Remains Problematic – and a Tentative Corpus-driven Solution. *Proceedings of the Third International Conference, Europhras 2019, Computational and Corpus-Based Phraseology*, 145–156. https://doi.org/10.26615/978-2-9701095-6-3_020

Daems, J. (2022). Dutch literary translators' use and perceived usefulness of technology: The role of awareness and attitude. In Hadley, James and Taivalkoski-Shilov, Kristiina and Teixeira, Carlos and Toral, Antonio (Ed.), *Using Technologies for Creative-Text Translation* (pp. 40–65). Routledge.

Eder, M., Rybicki, J., & Kestemont, M. (2016). Stylometry with R: A Package for Computational Text Analysis. *The R Journal*, *8*(1), 107–121.

Guerberof-Arenas, A., & Toral, A. (2020). The impact of post-editing and machine translation on creativity and reading experience. *Translation Spaces*, *9*(2), 255–282. https://doi.org/10.1075/ts.20035.gue

Guerberof-Arenas, A., & Toral, A. (2022). Creativity in translation: Machine translation as a constraint for literary texts. *Translation Spaces*, *11*(2), 184–212. https://doi.org/10.1075/ts.21025.gue

Guerberof-Arenas, A., & Toral, A. (2024). To be or not to be: A translation reception study of a literary text translated into Dutch and Catalan using machine translation. *Target. International Journal of Translation Studies*, *36*(2), 215–244. https://doi.org/10.1075/target.22134.gue

Hadley, J. L., Taivalkoski-Shilov, K., Teixeira, C. S. C., & Toral, A. (Eds.). (2022). *Using Technologies for Creative-Text Translation*. Routledge. https://doi.org/10.4324/9781003094159

Qi, P., Zhang, Y., Zhang, Y., Bolton, J., & Manning, C. D. (2020). *Stanza: A Python Natural Language Processing Toolkit for Many Human Languages* (arXiv:2003.07082). arXiv. https://doi.org/10.48550/arXiv.2003.07082

Ruffo, P. (2021). *In-between role and technology: Literary translators on navigating the new socio-technological paradigm.* Heriot-Watt University.

Tavecchio, L. M. (2010). *Sentence patterns in English and Dutch: A contrastive corpus analysis* [PhD-Thesis - Research and graduation internal]. LOT.

Terribile, S. (2023). Is post-editing really faster than human translation? *Translation Spaces*. https://doi.org/10.1075/ts.22044.ter

Toral, A. (2019). Post-editese: An Exacerbated Translationese. In M. Forcada, A. Way, B. Haddow, & R. Sennrich (Eds.), *Proceedings of Machine Translation Summit XVII: Research Track* (pp. 273–281). European Association for Machine Translation. https://aclanthology.org/W19-6627

Toral, A., & Way, A. (2018). What Level of Quality Can Neural Machine Translation Attain on Literary Text? In J. Moorkens, S. Castilho, F. Gaspari, & S. Doherty (Eds.), *Translation Quality Assessment: From Principles to Practice* (pp. 263–287). Springer International Publishing. https://doi.org/10.1007/978-3-319-91241-7_12

Vanmassenhove, E., Shterionov, D., & Way, A. (2019). Lost in Translation: Loss and Decay of Linguistic Richness in Machine Translation. In M. Forcada, A. Way, B. Haddow, & R. Sennrich (Eds.), *Proceedings of Machine Translation Summit XVII: Research Track* (pp. 222–232). European Association for Machine Translation. https://aclanthology.org/W19-6622

Vanroy, B., Clercq, O. D., Tezcan, A., Daems, J., & Macken, L. (2021). Metrics of Syntactic Equivalence to Assess Translation Difficulty. In M. Carl (Ed.), *Explorations in Empirical Translation Process Research* (pp. 259–294).

Springer International Publishing. https://doi.org/10.1007/978-3-030-69777-8_10

Webster, R., Fonteyne, M., Tezcan, A., Macken, L., & Daems, J. (2020). Gutenberg goes neural: Comparing features of Dutch human translations with raw neural machine translation outputs in a corpus of English literary classics. *INFORMATICS-BASEL*, *7*(3), 21.

Winters, M., & Kenny, D. (2023). Mark My Keywords. In A. Rothwell, A. Way, & R. Youdale, *Computer-Assisted Literary Translation* (1st ed., pp. 69–88). Routledge. https://doi.org/10.4324/9781003357391-5

Zhai, Y., Max, A., & Vilnat, A. (2018). Construction of a Multilingual Corpus Annotated with Translation Relations. In P. Machonis, A. Barreiro, K. Kocijan, & M. Silberztein (Eds.), *Proceedings of the First Workshop on Linguistic Resources for Natural Language Processing* (pp. 102–111). Association for Computational Linguistics. https://aclanthology.org/W18-3814

Machine Translation Meets Large Language Models: Evaluating ChatGPT's Ability to Automatically Post-Edit Literary Texts

Lieve Macken
LT[3], Language and Translation Technology Team
Ghent University
Belgium
lieve.macken@ugent.be

Abstract

Large language models such as GPT-4 have been trained on vast corpora, giving them excellent language understanding. This study explores the use of ChatGPT for post-editing machine translations of literary texts. Three short stories, machine translated from English into Dutch, were post-edited by 7-8 professional translators and ChatGPT. Automatic metrics were used to evaluate the number and type of edits made, and semantic and syntactic similarity between the machine translation and the corresponding post-edited versions. A manual analysis classified errors in the machine translation and changes made by the post-editors. The results show that ChatGPT made more changes than the average post-editor. ChatGPT improved lexical richness over machine translation for all texts. The analysis of editing types showed that ChatGPT replaced more words with synonyms, corrected fewer machine errors and introduced more problems than professionals.

1 Introduction

In recent years, there has been a noticeable shift in the perception of the use of computer-assisted translation technologies for literary translation. Advances in the quality of machine translation (MT) and the development of sophisticated computer-assisted translation (CAT) tools have contributed to this changing landscape (Rothwell et al., 2023).

Following the emergence of neural machine translation, a growing body of research has examined the use of Machine Translation (MT) and Post-Editing (PE) for literary texts. Researchers have looked at various aspects related to the use of MT and PE in the context of literary translation, such as perceived usefulness of MT (Moorkens et al., 2018; Şahin and Gürses, 2021; Daems, 2022; Ruffo, 2022), ethical issues (Taivalkoski-Shilov, 2019; Kenny and Winters, 2020; Li, 2023), translation quality (Webster et al., 2020; Macken et al., 2022; Castilho and Resende, 2022), the impact on the translation process (Toral et al., 2018; Kolb, 2023), and the reader's reception of the final product (Guerberof-Arenas and Toral, 2020).

Further automation of the translation process can be accomplished by implementing Automatic Post-Editing (APE), which refers to methods that improve the output of machine translation systems by applying automatic editing operations (do Carmo et al., 2021). Technological advances are rapidly evolving and the potential of using AI systems based on large language models (e.g. ChatGPT) is currently being explored for a variety of applications (Guimarães et al., 2024), one of which is the post-editing of machine translation output (Raunak et al., 2023).

This study explores ChatGPT's ability to automatically post-edit literary texts that were machine-translated from English into Dutch by a neural machine translation system. We evaluate ChatGPT's performance by comparing its automatically post-edited texts to versions that were post-edited by professional literary translators.

2 Related research

Over the past decade, a number of studies have been carried out to examine the usefulness and

Proceedings of the 1st Workshop on Creative-text Translation and Technology, pages 65–81
June 27, 2024 ©2024 European Association for Machine Translation

suitability of machine translation and post-editing for literary translation. Researchers often compare raw (unedited) machine translations of literary texts with their (published) human-translated counterparts. The MT systems used are either generic systems (Webster et al., 2020; Hu and Li, 2023) or MT systems adapted specially for literary translation (Toral et al., 2024; Matusov, 2019; Toral et al., 2024).

In order to gain valuable insights into the strengths and limitations of MT for literary translation, error classification schemes such as MQM (Lommel et al., 2014) or SCATE (Tezcan et al., 2017) are often used. These classification schemes typically distinguish between accuracy and fluency errors. Accuracy errors refer to the failure to transfer meaning correctly from source to target, whereas fluency errors refer to the failure to produce grammatically correct, idiomatic and fluent translations. Existing error classification schemes have been adapted to suit the specific characteristics of literary texts (Tezcan et al., 2019; Matusov, 2019).

Despite the high quality of the current generation of transformer-based neural MT systems, they still produce errors in both accuracy and fluency. This is certainly the case with more creative use of language, which is typical of literary texts. In addition, machine-translated texts exhibit different linguistic characteristics (e.g. less lexical variety, less cohesion, syntactically less diverse texts) than human translations (Vanmassenhove et al., 2019; Webster et al., 2020). The involvement of professional translators in the translation of literary texts is therefore essential.

In the context of literary translation, post-editing can be applied by having human translators work on the raw machine translation suggestions (Toral et al., 2018; Şahin and Gürses, 2019; Guerberof-Arenas and Toral, 2020; Castilho and Resende, 2022; Kolb, 2023). Human translators then correct the errors and polish the machine's raw output, transforming it into a high-quality, publishable literary translation by ensuring that the translated texts capture the nuances, cultural references, and literary techniques present in the original work.

In their study, Macken et al. (2022) compared three successive versions of a Dutch translation of an English novel: the raw MT output, the post-edited version and the revision of the post-edited text. They manually annotated the errors in the MT and categorised the editing changes in accordance with a linguistic typology. The study showed that most MT errors were corrected in the post-editing process, and that the post-editor mainly made lexico-semantic and stylistic changes. Forty-four percent of the post-editing changes involved the correction of MT errors, 24% were preferred changes and 9% were labelled as 'undesirable'.

They also used different automatic metrics to measure the (dis)similarity between the different versions, focusing on different aspects. The amount of editing was assessed by Translation Edit Rate (Snover et al., 2006) and CharCut (Lardilleux and Lepage, 2017). Semantic similarity was measured by the neural metrics COMET (Rei et al., 2020) and BERTScore (Zhang et al., 2019), which calculate the distance between vector representations of sentences and tokens. ASTrED (Vanroy et al., 2021), a metric that compares the edit distance between the dependency structures of two sentences, taking into account word alignment information, was used to quantify syntactic changes.

Another feature that has been widely studied in previous research on literary machine translation is lexical richness. Vanmassenhove et al. (2019) showed that MT systems are not able to achieve the same level of lexical richness as human translated texts. Webster et al. (2020) also observed a decrease in lexical richness from human translation to machine translation, suggesting a certain homogenisation of the lexicon used by NMT systems. Macken et al. (2022) investigated whether the level of lexical richness increases during post-editing and revision, but in their study they found similar levels of lexical richness in the MT, PE and revised translation.

Large language models such as GPT-4 or LLaMA are trained on unprecedentedly large corpora. LLaMA-3 for example has been pre-trained on approximately 15 trillion tokens of text gathered from publicly available sources[1]. Due to the size of the training set, they have a comprehensive understanding of language. As they are trained on a much larger data set than other end-user applications such as automatic speech recognition or machine translation, researchers propose a combination of the two. Radhakrishnan et al. (2023) used LLaMA to correct errors produced by the Whisper automatic speech recognition system (Radford et al., 2023), a task similar to the post-editing of

[1] https://ai.meta.com/blog/meta-llama-3/

machine translation output.

Raunak et al. (2023) explore the use of GPT-4 for automatic post-editing of NMT output in different language pairs. They experimented with WMT-22 General MT translation task datasets and WMT-20 and WMT-21 News translation task submissions annotated with MQM. Translation quality was assessed using neural evaluation metrics. Their results show that GPT-4 effectively improves translation quality compared to the best systems from WMT-22 across a number of language pairs and generates meaningful edits to translations. But they also show that GPT-4 can produce hallucinated edits, suggesting caution in its use as an expert translation post-editor.

Research on the use of ChatGPT for automatic post-editing is very scarce and has not yet been applied to challenging text types such as literary texts. In this study, we extend the work of Raunak et al. (2023) and use ChatGPT 4.0 to automatically post-edit more creative texts. We are not only interested in whether automatic post-editing with ChatGPT improves the quality of the neural machine translation output. We also want to know how ChatGPT's post-editing ability compares with that of professional literary translators. Using automatic and manual evaluation methods we seek an answer to the following research questions

- RQ1: Does ChatGPT make more or less changes to the machine-translated texts than professional literary translators?
- RQ2: To what extent does ChatGPT preserve the meaning of the text compared to professional literary translators?
- RQ3: Does ChatGPT make different types of changes to the machine-translated texts than professional literary translators?
- RQ4: Does ChatGPT solve all the errors present in the machine-translated texts? Does it introduce new problems?

3 Methodology

3.1 Data

We use part of the data set collected in the DUAL-T project (Ruffo et al., 2023; Ruffo et al., 2024), which compares three different literary translation conditions: the conventional method using a word processing tool (Microsoft Word), translation within a computer-assisted translation environment (Trados Studio 2022), and post-editing of machine translation output. Three short stories were selected from the short story collection 'One More Thing' by the American writer B. J. Novak[2].

A total of twenty-three professional literary translators (8 male, 15 female) participated in the DUAL-T experiments. The translators were contacted through professional translator associations in Flanders and The Netherlands and they were paid to take part in the study. Years of experience in translating literary texts ranged from 1 year to 43 years. Eight participants had made use of post-editing in their professional translation work. Each translator translated each of the three texts into Dutch in a different condition. They were instructed to produce translations of publishable quality. Each combination of text and condition appeared the same number of times in the entire data set.

In this study, we only use the post-edited versions of the three texts. The machine translations of the three texts were generated in July 2023 using a commercial neural machine translation system (DeepL). The professional literary translators worked in a proprietary web-based platform that displayed the source and the machine-translated target text side by side. During translation, the translators could consult online resources when they felt it was appropriate. The source text characteristics and the number of post-edited versions of the three texts are presented in Table 1.

	Words	Sentences	Post-edited versions
T1	306	30	7
T2	349	27	8
T3	290	30	8

Table 1: Source text characteristics of the three short stories and number of texts post-edited by professional literary translators

We slightly adapted the system and user prompts of Raunak et al. (2023) to generate the post-edited versions of ChatGPT 4.0. The system prompt contains the initial instruction to ChatGPT to complete the post-editing task. The user prompts were given three times, one for each text. The prompts we used for the experiments are presented in Appen-

[2]A published translation of this collection is available in Dutch, but only as a printed book. It is therefore very unlikely that this Dutch translation was used to train chatGPT.

dices A and B.

3.2 Automatic evaluation

We use various automatic metrics to evaluate and compare all post-edited versions of each text. Before calculating the automatic metrics, all texts were tokenized using the Stanza toolkit (Qi et al., 2020) and manually aligned at sentence level.

To quantify the amount of editing done by each post-editor, we compare the machine-translated texts with the post-edited versions of each professional translator and ChatGPT. We use Translation Edit Rate (TER) (Snover et al., 2006) and CharCut (Lardilleux and Lepage, 2017). TER quantifies editing operations at the token level, while CharCut works at the character level. As such Charcut is more lenient and penalises the use of different word forms (e.g. the Dutch word *stad* (En: *town*) had been changed to the diminutive *stadje* (En: *small town*)) to a lesser extent than TER. TER scores were obtained via the MATEO platform[3] (Vanroy et al., 2023). For CharCut, we used the Python code available on GitHub[4].

We used BERTScore (Zhang et al., 2019) to measure the semantic similarity between the machine-translated texts and each of their post-edited versions. BERTScore is an automatic evaluation metric for text generation, which uses contextual embeddings to compute a similarity score for two given sentences. As such, it can capture semantic similarity of synonyms and will give a higher score to sentences that are semantically similar (e.g. *van de plank – van een rek* (En: *from the shelf – from a rack*) than sentences in which the content has been changed, (e.g. *van de plank – uit een kast* (En: *from the shelf – from a cupboard*). BERTScores were also obtained via the MATEO platform.

Webster et al. (2020) observed that MT systems tend to follow the syntactic structure of the source text more closely than human translators. We assume that the post-editors will therefore adapt the syntactic structure to bring it closer to the norms of the target language. We use ASTrED[5] (Vanroy et al., 2021) to quantify the degree of similarity between the syntactic structure of the machine-translated texts and each of their post-edited versions. ASTrED computes the edit distance between the dependency structures of two sentences, taking into account word alignment information. Under the hood, ASTrED uses the stanza parser (Qi et al., 2020) for the creation of universal dependency trees and AWESOME-align (Dou and Neubig, 2021) for word alignment. It assigns a lower score to sentences with a more similar dependency structure than to sentences where the structure has changed more. In the example in Figure 1, the human post-editor made only minimal changes to the structure, whereas ChatGPT made more changes to the structure. The resulting ASTrED scores are resp. 0,13 for the human post-edited sentence and 0,26 for ChatGPT's version.

Finally, to assess the lexical diversity of each post-edited text, we calculated the Moving Average Type-Token Ratio with a window size of 50 (MATTR-50)[6]. MATTR calculates the ratio of different unique words (types) to the total number of words (tokens) using a moving window of predefined word length and is therefore not sensitive to differences in text length. To obtain more accurate results, we lower-cased all texts before calculating MATTR.

3.3 Manual evaluation

For the manual evaluation, we largely follow the methodology of Macken et al. (2022). We annotate all errors in the MT output and classify all post-editing changes in the subsequent post-edited translations. As the manual annotation of post-editing changes is very time-consuming, we only annotated the ChatGPT version and the post-edited texts produced by the three most experienced professional translators for each text. The translators' years of experience were 24, 21 and 10 for text 1, 43, 20 and 15 for text 2 and 28, 8 and 8 for text 3.

To evaluate the quality of the machine translation, the three machine-translated texts were annotated according to an adapted version of the SCATE error taxonomy (Tezcan et al., 2019). We used the same reduced set of labels as in Macken et al. (2022).

We further classified all post-editing changes in the 4 post-edited versions per text from a linguistic perspective. We made minor adaptations to the categorisation scheme of Macken et al. (2022), which includes four main categories (*lexico-semantic*, *syntax & morphology*, *style* and *spelling & punc-*

[3] https://mateo.ivdnt.org/
[4] https://github.com/alardill/charcut
[5] https://github.com/BramVanroy/ASTrED
[6] https://github.com/kristopherkyle/lexical_diversity

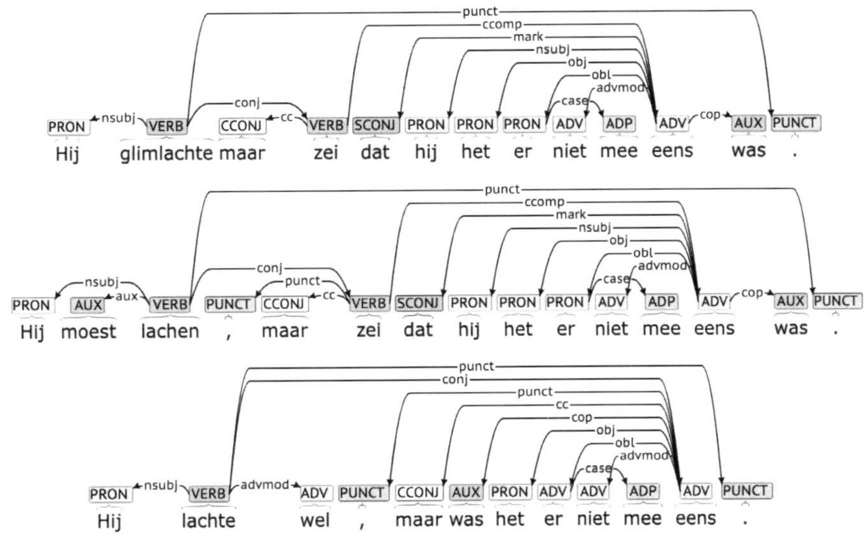

Figure 1: Universal Dependency Trees for the machine-translated sentence, and two post-edited sentences, resp. by a human post-editor and by ChatGPT. English source sentence: *He smiled but said he didn't agree.*

tuation), which are subdivided into subcategories (see Table 4 and Appendix C for more details). We also labelled each post-editing change in terms of correctness and necessity by using the following labels (*MT error correction, consistency, preferential* and *undesirable change*). Undesirable changes are edits that clearly degrade the quality of the translation. In the final translation we also identified any MT errors that were not fixed.

All annotations were done in Excel by the author of the paper. To facilitate the labelling of post-editing changes, we used Charcut (Lardilleux and Lepage, 2017), which produces an HTML document visualizing the differences between the MT output and the PE version, see Figure 2. The annotation guidelines are given in Appendix C.

Figure 2: Example of Charcut visualizations (MT–APE)

4 Results

4.1 Automatic evaluation

Table 2 shows the results of the four automatic metrics quantifying the amount of editing that took place (CharCut and TER), semantic similarity (BERTScore) and syntactic similarity (ASTrED). The metrics were calculated on all translations available to us. The table summarises the results per condition: APE represents the results of the automatically post-edited text by ChatGPT, while PE is the average of the 7 or 8 human post-edited versions.

		CharCut ↓	TER ↓	BERTScore ↑	ASTrED ↓
T1	APE	0,31	0,42	89,33	**0,22**
T1	PE	**0,26**	**0,36**	**90,57**	0,24
T2	APE	0,37	0,47	88,58	0,23
T2	PE	**0,24**	**0,34**	**91,46**	**0,18**
T3	APE	0,31	0,39	88,68	0,27
T3	PE	**0,17**	**0,24**	**93,07**	**0,18**

Table 2: Overview of automatic evaluation results per text. Up arrow: higher value means more similar; down arrow: lower value means more similar.

If we compare ChatGPT with the 'average human post-editor', we see that ChatGPT makes more changes to the machine-translated texts than the average human post-editor. The results show a higher degree of editing, both in terms of CharCut and TER, a lower semantic similarity and, for two texts, also a lower syntactic similarity.

Figure 3 presents the CharCut and ASTrED

scores per text and per participant. For texts 2 and 3, ChatGPT obtains the highest CharCut scores. For text 1, two professional literary translators (P07 and P11) make more changes to the machine translation. ChatGPT's ASTrED score for texts 2 and 3 is the second highest; for text 1 it is in the middle range.

Figure 4 presents the MATTR-50 scores for the English source texts, the machine-translated texts and all post-edited versions. While English and Dutch MATTR-50 values cannot be directly compared due to different word formation rules (compounds are written as one word in Dutch), the MATTR-50 values of the English source texts can be used as benchmark to interpret the other values. In most cases, post-editing results in higher MATTR-50 values. ChatGPT achieves higher MATTR-50 values for all texts, increasing the level of lexical richness compared to the machine-translated texts.

4.2 Manual evaluation

All errors were manually annotated in the machine-translated texts. Overall, the quality of the commercial neural machine translation system is relatively good, with only 18 accuracy errors and 29 fluency errors. Table 3 gives an overview of all the errors found in the machine-translated texts.

In terms of accuracy, mistranslations make up the largest group of errors. Examples of accuracy errors are wrong translations of single words (e.g. *scraggly* is translated as *schamele* (En: *poor, scanty*)) or expressions (e.g. *on the last day the rain cleared* is translated literally as *op de laatste dag klaarde de regen op*, which is not idiomatic in Dutch).

The other major group of problems are style problems, and in particular disfluent sentences (belonging to the 'fluency' category). Disfluent sentence constructions are most often the result of copying the structure of the source sentences too literally, as is the case in the following example: *De plek waar mensen hun hele leven voor gespaard hebben om naartoe te gaan*, which is a rather literal translation of *The place that people saved up to visit their whole lives*.

Table 4 gives an overview of all post-editing changes in the three texts. In total, 751 post-editing changes were annotated. Most post-editing changes are lexico-semantic (69%) or stylistic (20%) changes.

Accuracy	**18**	**Fluency**	**29**
Mistranslation	16	Coherence	2
Multiword	5	Discourse marker	0
Word sense	2	Coreference	1
Other	9	Tense	0
Addition	0	Other	1
Omission	0	Lexicon	7
Untranslated	2	Grammar & syntax	1
Do not translate	0	Style	16
		Disfluent	12
		Repetition	1
		Other	3
		Spelling & punctuation	3
		Capitalisation	0
		Compound	1
		Punctuation	2
		Other	0

Table 3: Accuracy and fluency errors in the three machine-translated texts

Post-editors often replace words with synonyms (*boekwinkel → boekhandel (En: bookstore)*), make words or phrases more explicit or specific (*plek → stad (En: place → town)*), make them more implicit or vague (*hij tekende zelfs een diagram → hij tekende het zelfs uit (En: He even drew a diagram → he even drew it); in de stad → in de buurt (En: in the city → in the neigbourhood)*), or replace words or phrases from the MT output with a better collocation or more idiomatic expression (*klaarde de regen op → klaarde het op (En: the rain cleared); op zijn laatst om → of uiterlijk (En: at the latest)*).

Post-editors also often make improvements to the structure of the machine translation, e.g. *(De plek waar mensen hun hele leven voor gespaard hebben om naartoe te gaan → Sommige mensen spaarden hun hele leven om er een keer naartoe te gaan (En: The place that people saved up to visit their whole lives → Some people saved their whole lives to go there once))*. They also often prefer another word order *(om bloemen te kopen voor zijn vrouw → om bloemen voor zijn vrouw te kopen (En: to pick up flowers for his wife))* or make other stylistisc changes *(een vage en opgeblazen en maffe lach → een vage opgeblazen gekke glimlach (En: a vague and bloated and goofy smile))*.

Most of the spelling and punctuation changes are related to changing double quotes by single quotes.

Table 5 shows the breakdown of the lexico-semantic and stylistic edits per text and per post-editor. For each of the texts, we can see quite

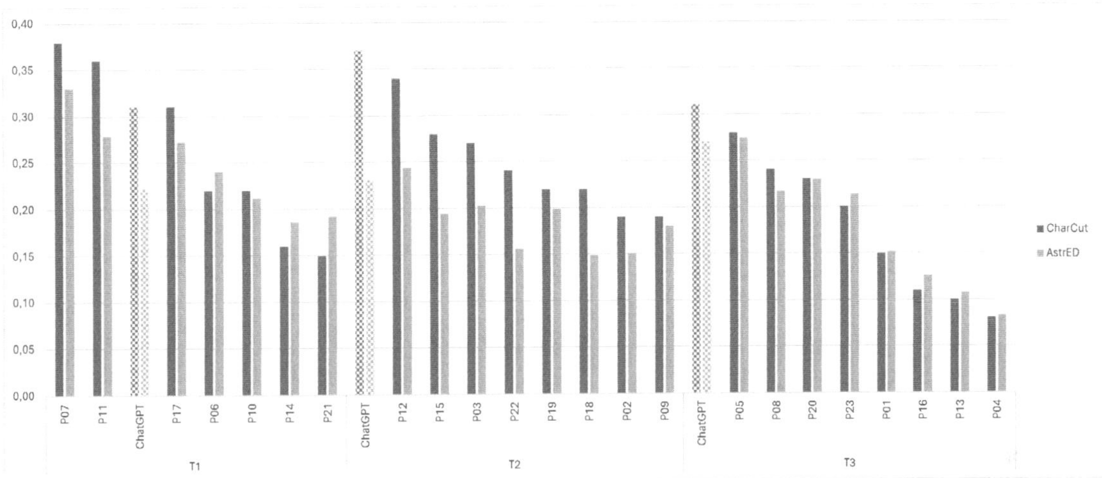

Figure 3: CharCut and ASTrED scores per text per participant, ordered by CharCut scores

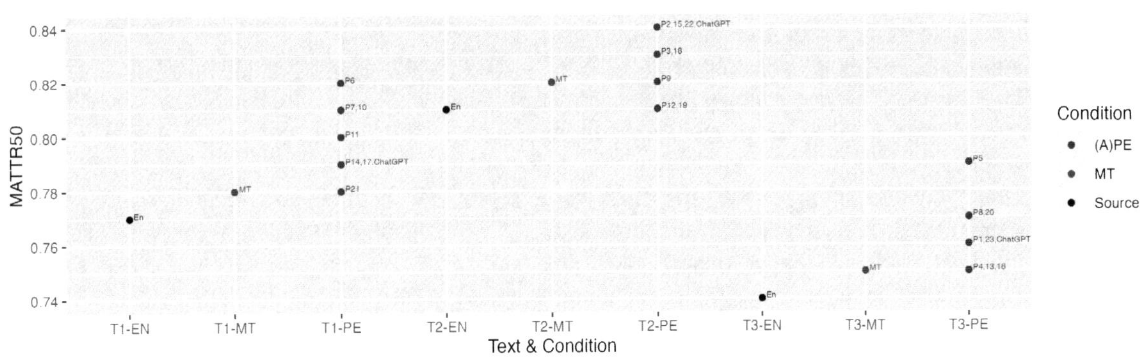

Figure 4: MATTR-50 scores for the English source text, the MT the and (automatically) post-edited texts

Lexico-semantic	517	Syntax & morphology	26
Addition	2	Agreement	2
Coherence marker	39	Number	3
Collocation & idiom	128	Diminutive	8
Deletion	16	Tense	10
Explicitation & specific	68	Other	3
Implicitation & vague	46		
Synonym	134		
Other	84		
Spelling & punctuation	**58**	**Style**	**150**
Capitalization	0	Word order	37
Compound	2	Structural change	50
Linking word & punctuation	9	Shorter	15
Punctuation added	8	Split sentence	0
Punctuation deleted	2	Merged sentence	3
Other	37	Other	45

Table 4: Categorisation of all post-editing changes in the three texts

a few differences in both the number of changes and the types of changes made by each of the post-editors. The most striking difference between ChatGPT and professional literary translators is that ChatGPT makes more lexico-semantic changes, which can be attributed to the subcategory 'synonym'. ChatGPT thus replaces words with synonyms more often than professional literary translators.

Table 6 presents the quality labels assigned to all post-editing changes by the three post-editors and ChatGPT. The majority of changes (71%) are preferential in nature; 20% of all changes are corrections of MT errors; 5% of the changes were for consistency reasons (e.g. because of adaptations made earlier in the text) and 3% of the changes were labelled as 'undesirable'. These last changes either introduced new errors or made the final target text inconsistent with the information in the source text. Most of the MT errors (80% of all accuracy errors and 88% of all fluency errors) present in the machine-translated texts were solved during post-editing.

The distribution of quality labels is slightly different for ChatGPT compared to the three post-editors, with 74% preferential changes (vs. 70%), 18% MT error corrections (vs. 21%), 6% undesirable changes (vs. 2%) and 2% changes to make the text consistent (vs. 6%). This means that ChatGPT corrects fewer MT errors and introduces more problems than the human post-editors. An example of problem introduced by ChatGPT is presented in Figure 5. In the example, the MT produces a literal translation of the phrase *In the end, this one wasn't for her*, which does not make sense in Dutch. ChatGPT adds the Dutch word *plek*

TEXT 1	ChatGPT	P6	P11	P17
Lexico-semantic	**48**	**33**	**40**	**46**
Coherence marker	3	6	4	6
Collocation & idiom	13	10	16	12
Deletion	2	3	2	1
Synonym	15	2	4	9
Explicitation & specific	5	5	8	10
Implicitation & vague	5	5	3	1
Other	5	2	3	7
Style	**8**	**9**	**14**	**16**
Word order	4	1	3	4
Structural change	1	3	1	1
Shorter	2	1	4	0
Merged sentence	0	1	1	1
Other	1	3	5	10
TEXT 2	**ChatGPT**	**P2**	**P12**	**P15**
Lexico-semantic	**76**	**32**	**46**	**50**
Addition	2	0	0	0
Coherence marker	3	3	1	3
Collocation & idiom	11	11	15	12
Deletion	1	0	0	2
Synonym	33	8	7	9
Explicitation & specific	4	4	7	6
Implicitation & vague	8	1	4	5
Other	14	5	12	13
Style	**8**	**16**	**20**	**10**
Word order	3	5	3	2
Structural change	0	5	10	2
Shorter	1	1	1	1
Other	4	5	6	5
TEXT 3	**ChatGPT**	**P5**	**P16**	**P20**
Lexico-semantic	**46**	**45**	**19**	**36**
Coherence marker	3	4	0	3
Collocation & idiom	8	7	5	8
Deletion	3	2	0	0
Synonym	16	11	6	14
Explicitation & specific	7	7	2	3
Implicitation & vague	3	5	2	4
Other	6	9	4	4
Style	**19**	**15**	**4**	**11**
Word order	5	4	2	1
Structural change	9	9	2	7
Shorter	3	0	0	1
Other	2	2	0	2

Table 5: Overview of the lexico-semantic and stylistic edits per text and per post-editor

(En: place) so that the meaning of the sentence changes to *In the end, this place was not for her.*

T02_EN.tok.sent.txt
In the end , this one wasn't for her .

T02_MT.tok.sent.txt
Uiteindelijk was deze niet voor haar .

T02_ChatGPT4.tok.sent.txt
Op het einde was deze plek toch niet voor haar bestemd .

Figure 5: Example of an undesirable edit by ChatGPT

Quality label	All	Post-editors	ChatGPT
Preferential	536 (71%)	367 (70%)	169 (74%)
MT error correction	153 (20%)	112 (21%)	41 (18%)
Consistency	37 (5%)	33 (6%)	4 (2%)
Undesirable	25 (3%)	10 (2%)	15 (6%)

Table 6: Overview of the quality labels assigned to all post-editing changes by the three post-editors and ChatGPT

5 Discussion

We conducted an experiment comparing the post-editing capabilities of ChatGPT with those of experienced professional literary translators working on English-Dutch literary texts. We used a data set collected in the DUAL-T project, in which 23 professional English-Dutch literary translators post-edited the neural machine translations of three short stories by the same author. We then asked ChatGPT 4.0 to create post-edited versions of the three texts. This collection of post-edited literary translations allows us to compare the results of human and automatic post-editing.

We formulated four research questions and used a combination of automatic and manual evaluation methods to compare all post-edited texts. The CharCut and TER results show that ChatGPT makes more changes to the machine-translated texts than the 'average human post-editor' (RQ1). ChatGPT achieved the highest CharCut scores for two texts and made the most lexico-semantic changes in all texts compared to the human post-editors. ChatGPT improved lexical richness over the machine translation for all texts. The obtained BERTScore values indicate that the meaning of the text is less preserved in ChatGPT's versions compared to those of the 'average professional literary translator' (RQ2).

When analysing the types of changes made by post-editors, we clearly see that post-editors mainly make lexico-semantic and stylistic changes, as was the case in Macken et al.'s study (2022). Looking more closely at the types of changes made by individual post-editors, we can see that there is a great deal of variation between different post-editors. A high degree of individual variation between professional translators during revision has been observed in previous studies (Daems and Macken, 2020) and can be attributed to the individual style of professional translators. The only striking difference between ChatGPT and professional literary translators is that it replaces words with synonyms more often than human post-editors (RQ3).

With only 18 accuracy errors and 29 fluency errors, the neural machine translation system did an excellent job. Most errors were solved during post-editing. Looking at the MT quality labels, we can conclude that ChatGPT solves fewer errors in the machine-translated texts and introduces more problems compared to professional literary translators (RQ4).

This study aimed to provide insights into the capabilities and limitations of ChatGPT for automatic post-editing of literary machine translation. Overall, ChatGPT proved to be a more aggressive post-editor than the professionals, making too many changes to the machine-translated text, despite being explicitly instructed not to do so in the prompt ("Do not edit the translation if the translation is faithful to the meaning of the source text and faithful to the style of the original author"). It also corrected fewer errors, introduced more problems and deviated more from the meaning of the target text. Nevertheless, ChatGPT corrected most of the errors and provided meaningful edits.

While fully automatic post-editing with ChatGPT is not yet feasible, and probably not desirable from an ethical point of view, AI tools based on large language models can generate high-quality post-editing suggestions. As such, they can certainly complement the toolkits of professional translators. A promising direction that deserves further investigation is to have human translators work directly on texts that have been automatically post-edited by AI. This could help to leverage the strengths of both human and machine skills.

References

Castilho, Sheila and Natália Resende. 2022. Post-editese in literary translations. *Information*, 13(2):66.

Daems, Joke and Lieve Macken. 2020. Post-editing human translations and revising machine translations : impact on efficiency and quality. In Koponen, Maarit, Brian Mossop, Isabelle Robert, and Giovanna Scocchera, editors, *Translation revision and/or post-editing : industry practices and cognitive processes*, pages 50–70. Routledge.

Daems, Joke. 2022. Dutch literary translators' use and perceived usefulness of technology : the role of awareness and attitude. In Hadley, James Luke, Kristiina Taivalkoski-Shilov, Carlos Teixeira, and Antonio Toral, editors, *Using technologies for creative-text translation*, Routledge Advances in

Translation and Interpreting Studies, pages 40–65. Routledge.

do Carmo, Félix, Dimitar Shterionov, Joss Moorkens, Joachim Wagner, Murhaf Hossari, Eric Paquin, Dag Schmidtke, Declan Groves, and Andy Way. 2021. A review of the state-of-the-art in automatic post-editing. *Machine Translation*, 35:101–143.

Dou, Zi-Yi and Graham Neubig. 2021. Word alignment by fine-tuning embeddings on parallel corpora. In Merlo, Paola, Jorg Tiedemann, and Reut Tsarfaty, editors, *Proceedings of the 16th Conference of the European Chapter of the Association for Computational Linguistics: Main Volume*, pages 2112–2128, Online, April. Association for Computational Linguistics.

Guerberof-Arenas, Ana and Antonio Toral. 2020. The impact of post-editing and machine translation on creativity and reading experience. *Translation Spaces*, 9(2):255–282.

Guimarães, Nuno, Ricardo Campos, and Alípio Jorge. 2024. Pre-trained language models: What do they know? *Wiley Interdisciplinary Reviews: Data Mining and Knowledge Discovery*, 14(1):e1518.

Hu, Kaibao and Xiaoqian Li. 2023. The creativity and limitations of ai neural machine translation: A corpus-based study of deepl's english-to-chinese translation of shakespeare's plays. *Babel*, 69(4):546–563.

Kenny, Dorothy and Marion Winters. 2020. Machine translation, ethics and the literary translator's voice. *Translation Spaces*, 9(1):123–149.

Kolb, Waltraud. 2023. 'I Am a Bit Surprised': Literary Translation and Post-Editing Processes Compared. In Rothwell, Andrew, Andy Way, and Roy Youdale, editors, *Computer-Assisted Literary Translation*, pages 53–68. Routledge.

Lardilleux, Adrien and Yves Lepage. 2017. Charcut: Human-targeted character-based mt evaluation with loose differences. In *Proceedings of the 14th International Conference on Spoken Language Translation*, pages 146–153.

Li, Bo. 2023. Ethical issues for literary translation in the era of artificial intelligence. *Babel*, 69(4):529–545.

Lommel, Arle, Hans Uszkoreit, and Aljoscha Burchardt. 2014. Multidimensional quality metrics (mqm): A framework for declaring and describing translation quality metrics. *Tradumàtica*, (12):455–463.

Macken, Lieve, Bram Vanroy, Luca Desmet, and Arda Tezcan. 2022. Literary translation as a three-stage process: machine translation, post-editing and revision. In *Proceedings of the 23rd Annual Conference of the European Association for Machine Translation*, pages 101–110, Ghent, Belgium, June. European Association for Machine Translation.

Matusov, Evgeny. 2019. The challenges of using neural machine translation for literature. In Hadley, James, Maja Popović, Haithem Afli, and Andy Way, editors, *Proceedings of the Qualities of Literary Machine Translation*, pages 10–19, Dublin, Ireland, August. European Association for Machine Translation.

Moorkens, Joss, Antonio Toral, Sheila Castilho, and Andy Way. 2018. Translators' perceptions of literary post-editing using statistical and neural machine translation. *Translation Spaces*, 7(2):240–262.

Qi, Peng, Yuhao Zhang, Yuhui Zhang, Jason Bolton, and Christopher D. Manning. 2020. Stanza: A python natural language processing toolkit for many human languages. In Celikyilmaz, Asli and Tsung-Hsien Wen, editors, *Proceedings of the 58th Annual Meeting of the Association for Computational Linguistics: System Demonstrations*, pages 101–108, Online, July. Association for Computational Linguistics.

Radford, Alec, Jong Wook Kim, Tao Xu, Greg Brockman, Christine Mcleavey, and Ilya Sutskever. 2023. Robust speech recognition via large-scale weak supervision. In Krause, Andreas, Emma Brunskill, Kyunghyun Cho, Barbara Engelhardt, Sivan Sabato, and Jonathan Scarlett, editors, *Proceedings of the 40th International Conference on Machine Learning*, volume 202 of *Proceedings of Machine Learning Research*, pages 28492–28518. PMLR, 23–29 Jul.

Radhakrishnan, Srijith, Chao-Han Yang, Sumeer Khan, Rohit Kumar, Narsis Kiani, David Gomez-Cabrero, and Jesper Tegnér. 2023. Whispering LLaMA: A cross-modal generative error correction framework for speech recognition. In Bouamor, Houda, Juan Pino, and Kalika Bali, editors, *Proceedings of the 2023 Conference on Empirical Methods in Natural Language Processing*, pages 10007–10016, Singapore, December. Association for Computational Linguistics.

Raunak, Vikas, Amr Sharaf, Yiren Wang, Hany Awadalla, and Arul Menezes. 2023. Leveraging GPT-4 for automatic translation post-editing. In Bouamor, Houda, Juan Pino, and Kalika Bali, editors, *Findings of the Association for Computational Linguistics: EMNLP 2023*, pages 12009–12024, Singapore, December. Association for Computational Linguistics.

Rei, Ricardo, Craig Stewart, Ana C Farinha, and Alon Lavie. 2020. Comet: A neural framework for mt evaluation. In *Proceedings of the 2020 Conference on Empirical Methods in Natural Language Processing (EMNLP)*, pages 2685–2702.

Rothwell, Andrew, Andy Way, and Roy Youdale. 2023. *Computer-Assisted Literary Translation*. Taylor & Francis.

Ruffo, Paola, Joke Daems, and Lieve Macken. 2023. Developing user-centred approaches to technological innovation in literary translation (DUAL-T).

In *Proceedings of the 24th Annual Conference of the European Association for Machine Translation*, pages 491–492, Tampere, Finland, June. European Association for Machine Translation.

Ruffo, Paola, Joke Daems, and Lieve Macken. 2024. User testing of three literary translation workflows: measured vs perceived effort when using a word processor, a cat tool, and a machine translation postediting (MTPE) platform. Manuscript submitted for publication.

Ruffo, Paola. 2022. Collecting literary translators' narratives : towards a new paradigm for technological innovation in literary translation. In Hadley, James Luke, Kristiina Taivalkoski-Shilov, Carlos Teixeira, and Antonio Toral, editors, *Using technologies for creative-text translation*, Routledge Advances in Translation and Interpreting Studies, pages 18–39. Routledge.

Şahin, Mehmet and Sabri Gürses. 2019. Would MT kill creativity in literary retranslation? In Hadley, James, Maja Popović, Haithem Afli, and Andy Way, editors, *Proceedings of the Qualities of Literary Machine Translation*, pages 26–34, Dublin, Ireland, August. European Association for Machine Translation.

Şahin, Mehmet and Sabri Gürses. 2021. English-Turkish literary translation through human-machine interaction. *Tradumàtica tecnologies de la traducció*, (19):171–203.

Snover, Matthew, Bonnie Dorr, Richard Schwartz, Linnea Micciulla, and John Makhoul. 2006. A study of translation edit rate with targeted human annotation. In *Proceedings of the 7th Conference of the Association for Machine Translation in the Americas: Technical Papers*, pages 223–231.

Taivalkoski-Shilov, Kristiina. 2019. Ethical issues regarding machine(-assisted) translation of literary texts. *Perspectives*, 27(5):689–703.

Tezcan, Arda, Veronique Hoste, and Lieve Macken. 2017. Scate taxonomy and corpus of machine translation errors. In Pastor, Gloria Corpas and Isabel Durán-Muñoz, editors, *Trends in E-tools and resources for translators and interpreters*, volume 45 of *Approaches to Translation Studies*, pages 219–244. Brill — Rodopi.

Tezcan, Arda, Joke Daems, and Lieve Macken. 2019. When asport'is a person and other issues for nmt of novels. In *Machine Translation Summit XVII*, pages 40–49. European Association for Machine Translation.

Toral, Antonio, Martijn Wieling, and Andy Way. 2018. Post-editing effort of a novel with statistical and neural machine translation. *Frontiers in Digital Humanities*, 5.

Toral, Antonio, Andreas Van Cranenburgh, and Tia Nutters. 2024. Literary-adapted machine translation in a well-resourced language pair: Explorations with more data and wider contexts. In *Computer-Assisted Literary Translation*, pages 27–52. Routledge.

Vanmassenhove, Eva, Dimitar Shterionov, and Andy Way. 2019. Lost in translation: Loss and decay of linguistic richness in machine translation. In Forcada, Mikel, Andy Way, Barry Haddow, and Rico Sennrich, editors, *Proceedings of Machine Translation Summit XVII: Research Track*, pages 222–232, Dublin, Ireland, August. European Association for Machine Translation.

Vanroy, Bram, Orphée De Clercq, Arda Tezcan, Joke Daems, and Lieve Macken. 2021. Metrics of syntactic equivalence to assess translation difficulty. In Carl, Michael, editor, *Explorations in empirical translation process research*, volume 3 of *Machine Translation: Technologies and Applications*, pages 259–294. Springer.

Vanroy, Bram, Arda Tezcan, and Lieve Macken. 2023. MATEO: MAchine Translation Evaluation Online. In *Proceedings of the 24th Annual Conference of the European Association for Machine Translation*, pages 499–500, Tampere, Finland, June. European Association for Machine Translation.

Webster, Rebecca, Margot Fonteyne, Arda Tezcan, Lieve Macken, and Joke Daems. 2020. Gutenberg goes neural: Comparing features of Dutch human translations with raw neural machine translation outputs in a corpus of English literary classics. *Informatics*, 7(3):32.

Zhang, Tianyi, Varsha Kishore, Felix Wu, Kilian Q Weinberger, and Yoav Artzi. 2019. Bertscore: Evaluating text generation with bert. In *International Conference on Learning Representations*.

Appendix A. System prompt

You are a native Dutch speaker with a good working knowledge of English. You are also an experienced post-editor of literary translations from English into Dutch.

You know that every literary translation is a compromise between two goals: faithfulness to the meaning of the source text and faithfulness to the style of the original author.

"Faithfulness to the meaning of the source text" means that the meaning of the target text must not differ from that of the source text. In other words, no meaningful elements of the source text should be arbitrarily omitted, added or distorted in the Dutch translation.

Therefore, you will notice any deviations in the Dutch translations, including the following issues that make the given Dutch translation not optimal:

1. *Meaningful words in the English source text that are not rendered in the Dutch translation*
2. *Meaningful words in the Dutch translation that are not supported in the input*
3. *Words in the Dutch translation that do not convey the specific meaning of the corresponding word in the English source text*
4. *Words in the Dutch translation that are not in the correct language*

You will identify and correct the above problems in the Dutch translation, if present, in a way that improves the fluency of the translation.

"Faithfulness to the style of the original author" in literary translation implies that you sometimes have to think creatively to find solutions that are out of the ordinary, that go beyond the routine, while preserving the aesthetic intentions or effects that are evident in the source text.

You will identify any stylistic deviations in the Dutch translation, if present, in a way that improves the style of the translation.

Furthermore, as an expert translation post-editor, you will make sure that the following principles are followed when making improvements to the Dutch translation:

1. *Do not edit the translation if the translation is faithful to the meaning of the source text and faithful to the style of the original author*
2. *If the translation is very poor, generate an improved translation from scratch*
3. *No corrections are made that add words or phrases in the translation that are not supported in the English source text*
4. *Capitalization in the translation strictly follows capitalization in the input*
5. *The translation contains the appropriate articles and determiners to follow the specifics in the input*
6. *No meaningful words are left untranslated in the final, improved translation*
7. *Do not add any extraneous words, phrases, clauses or sentences to the translation that are not supported by the input*
8. *If the input begins with a non-capitalized word, the translation will begin with a non-capitalized word*
9. *Do not add end punctuations or full stops if they are not present in the source text*
10. *Do not assume that the source text contains typos; always err on the side of assuming that the presented input words are not typos*
11. *If the input contains offensive or obscene words, translate them faithfully*
12. *If the translation fails to convey the meaning of a large part of the input sentence, you include the translation for the missing part.*

Appendix B. User prompt

As an expert translation post editor, your task is to improve the Dutch translation for the below English text.

English text:

<English text comes here>

Dutch translation:

< Machine translation of the English text comes here>

Say "Improved Translation:". Then output the Dutch translation with proposed improvements that increase the faithfulness, fluency and style of the translation.

Appendix C. Manual annotation guidelines

Guidelines to annotate MT errors and post-editing changes

This manual annotation task consists of three separate subtasks:

1. Label all errors in the neural machine translation output according to predefined error taxonomy
2. Label all post-editing changes according to a predefined linguistic typology
3. Assess the necessity of the post-editing changes

To be able to assess the quality of a neural machine translation system all errors in the MT output will be indicated and labelled.

For each segment you will first label all accuracy and fluency errors according to a predefined error taxonomy.

En: It's fine, I was going to be heading that way anyway — I've been meaning to swing by Rome to get some garden shears, too. Anything else ? I can call you and check when I get to Rome."

MT: Geeft niet, ik was toch al van plan om die kant op te gaan. Ik wilde ook nog even langs Rome om een tuinschaar te halen. Verder nog iets? Ik kan je bellen en het controleren$_{[acc-mistra-ws]}$ als ik in Rome ben."

In a second step you label the post-editing changes. All post-editing changes will be categorized from two independent perspectives. You first classify the post-edits based on a text-linguistic typology. In a second assessment you judge the necessity of the post-edits in terms of translation quality. You decide whether the postedit was (1) necessary to correct an MT error or for consistency reasons, (2) could be considered a preferential change or (3) an undesirable/unneccessary edit.

To help you spot the differences between the MT output and the post-edited version or the post-edited and the revised version, you are provided with an html-document in which the differences are highlighted.

T01_EN.tok.sent.txt

I can call you and check when I get to Rome . "

T01_MT.tok.sent.txt

`Ik kan je bellen en het` **`controleren`** `als ik in Rome ben . "`

P10_WF03_T01.tok.sent.txt

`Ik kan je bellen en het` **`nog eens vragen`** `als ik in Rome ben . "`

Error taxonomy to annotate MT errors

ACCURACY ERRORS

mistra-mw	Mistranslation multiword: incorrect translation (often too literal) of a multi-word expression such as an idiom, a proverb, a collocation, a compound or a phrasal verb.
mistra-ws	Mistranslation word sense: incorrect translation. The MT refers to a different (and a wrong) sense of the source.
mistra-oth	Mistranslation other: incorrect translation (other cases)
dnt	Do not translate: source content is unnecessarily translated into target language when it should have been left untranslated.
untra	Untranslated: source text is not translated (but was copied to MT) when it should have been translated.
add	Addition: MT text that is not present in the source sentence.
omi	Omission: source content that cannot be found in MT.
cap-punct	Error related to capitalization or punctuation (not transferred correctly to the MT)

FLUENCY ERRORS

coh-disc	Coherence discourse marker: the conjunction or linking word expresses a strange relationship
coh-tense	Coherence tense: the tense of the verb is wrong/illogical in the context of the rest of the sentence/text
coh-coref	Coherence coreference: mismatch between entities, e.g. feminine pronoun to refer to a male person
coh-oth	Coherence other: other coherence problem (lack of logical structure, confusing relationships)
lex	Lexicon: lexical element does not entirely fit in the Dutch sentence
gra-synt	Grammar & syntax: anything that does not follow the grammatical or structural rules of the Dutch language
styl-disf	Style disfluent construction: The sentence / constituent is not grammatically incorrect, but it is nonetheless very difficult to read, it could be translated in a much more idiomatic way
styl-rep	Style repetition: the same or a very similar word/expression is used more than once
styl-oth	Style other: other stylistic or register-related problems
spel-comp	Spelling compound
spel-cap	Spelling capitalization
spel-oth	Spelling other
punct	Punctuation problem

Text-linguistic typology to annotate the post-editing/revision actions

LEXICO-SEMANTIC

add	Addition of a meaningful element (other than Lex-sem-coh or lex-sem-expl/spec)	Uiteindelijk was deze niet voor haar → uiteindelijk was deze plek niet voor haar
coh	A coherence marker has been added, or a pronoun or a conjunction has been replaced by a proper name or a more specific conjunction to improve the coherence of the text.	een bezinestation → zo'n benzinestation
expl-spec	Explicitation: information that could be derived from the source text and/or the MT output has been made explicit or the translation has become more specific, e.g. by using a hyponym	vliegtuigtijdschrift → een tijdschrift aan boord van een vliegtuig; om te halen → om te kopen
impl-vague	Implication: information has been made more implicit in the translation or the translation has become vaguer, e.g. by using a hyperonym	om zes uur → om zes; landkaarten → kaarten
del	Deletion: meaningful element of the source text or a relation that was present in both the ST and MT output has been deleted	Hij glimlachte maar zei dat hij het er niet mee eens was. → Hij lachte wel, maar was het er niet mee eens.
syn	Synonym: word or phrase from the MT output has been substituted for a synonym of that word/phrase	boekwinkel → boekhandel
coll-idiom	word or phrase from the MT output has been substituted for a better collocation or more idiomatic expression	klaarde de regen op → trok de regen weg; een of twee boeken → een boek of twee
other	Other lexico-semantic change	beter → aantrekkelijker

SYNTAX & MORPHOLOGY

agree	Agreement: change to solve an agreement problem	het soort … dat → de soort … die
number	Number: change in grammatical number (singular becomes plural and vice versa)	tuinschaar → tuinscharen
dim	Diminutive: change from base form to diminutive or vice versa	stad → stadje
tense	Tense: change of verb tense	heb gezien → had gezien
other	Other syntactic or morphological change	zou ze schuif → verplaatste ze

STYLE

order	Word order: the order of words has been altered	erin verdween → verdween erin
structural	Structural change: structural change to the MT output	wat vaak genoeg gebeurde → en dat gebeurde nogal eens
short	Shorter: the translation has become shorter / more concise	maakten wandelingen → wandelden
split	Split sentence: a MT sentence has been split into several sentences.	Wacht, wat is fauna? → Fauna? Wat is dat?
merge	Merged sentence: MT sentences have been merged into one sentence	Oké. Dat is prima. → Oké, goed hoor.
other	Other stylistic change	Ze keek naar alles → Zij keek naar alles.

SPELLING & PUNCTUATION

cap	Capitalization: change capitalization of a word	Kerstavond → kerstavond
cmp	Compound: correction of a wrongly spelled compound	tenminste → ten minste
lw-punct	Linking word & punctuation: replacement of a linking word by a punctuation mark or vice versa	, → en
add	Addition of a punctuation mark	terwijl → , terwijl
del	Deletion of a punctuation mark	prachtig, en → prachtig en
other	Other spelling or punctuation change	Veertig → '40; " → '

Categorization of post-editing changes from the perspective of correctness and necessity (translation quality)

MT-err	Edit to solve a problem indicated as an MT error.
Consist	Edit to achieve consistency between the segment and other segments in the text
Pref	Other (preferential) edits
Undes	Edits that deteriorate translation quality

Author Index